This book was presented to

....

on the occasion of

....

date

....

To my children, Sarah, Justyn, Jane,
Naomi, Duncan and Richard,
who all helped me to write this book

Many thanks, too, for the hours of help and expert advice given by Mary Wardrop and Martin Sutton, primary school teachers, the Reverend George Swannell who advised on theological aspects, Ann Frost who helped with language, and Oliver Styles, formerly of the Scripture Union.

Through-the-Bible
Storybook

Jennifer Rees Larcombe • Illustrated by Alan Parry

Zondervan Publishing House
Grand Rapids, Michigan

A Division of HarperCollins*Publishers*

First published in 1992 by Marshall Pickering.
Marshall Pickering is an imprint of HarperCollinsPublishers Ltd.,
77-85 Fulham Palace Road, Hammersmith, London W6 8JB, UK.

First published in the U.S. by ZondervanPublishingHouse
5300 Patterson, SE, Grand Rapids, Michigan, 49530

Library of Congress Cataloging–in–Publication Data

Rees, Jennifer.
    Through–the–Bible storybook / by Jennifer Rees.
        p.   cm.
    Summary: A collection of sixty Bible stories from the Old
Testament and forty from the New Testament.
        ISBN 0–310–56380–1
        1. Bible stories. English   (1. Bible stories.)
    BS551.2.R385   1992
    220.9' 505—dc20   91–42270
                                                                        CIP
                                                                        AC

Designed by Michael Leaman.
Typesetting by Michael Leaman Design Partnership.

Printed in Hong Kong.
ISBN 0551 02080 6 (UK).
ISBN 0-310-56380-1 (US).

INTRODUCTION

This project began when our six children grew tired of the inevitable "favorite" Bible stories and wanted to know what the Bible is really about. As I began to tell them the whole story at bedtime we discovered that it is simply the unfolding of God's secret plan for our welfare and happiness (Ephesians 1:9-10).

Although we tackled only one story each night we kept on recognizing themes, characters and places recurring frequently throughout the entire narrative. This, I believe, gave my children a sense of chronology and helped them to see where individual people and events actually fit in. It did far more than that, however; it helped us to see how God revealed himself to mankind, first by the choice of one man, one family, one nation, and finally by sending his Son. We could see how frequently the powers of darkness disrupted his great plan and how he continually drew people back again to himself through the judges, prophets and then by Jesus himself.

This book is arranged into one hundred short stories, each complete in itself; sixty in the Old Testament section and forty in the New. They have helped us as a family to know God in a real and more personal way and we hope you will enjoy and cherish them as much as we do.

CONTENTS

NEW TESTAMENT

THE DANGEROUS SNAKE

GOD WANTED FRIENDS; that is why he made people. First, of course, he had to make somewhere for them to live; people can't float about in nothing. So he began to make the world.

People need light, so he made the sun and the moon. He formed streams and lakes to give them water, and he knew they would need food so he gave them plants, fish, birds and animals.

God was pleased when he looked at it all. "Now I'm ready to make people," he said, so he planted a beautiful garden to be their home.

God called the first man and woman Adam and Eve, and each night he went down into the garden to talk to them. How happy they all were together and how much God enjoyed their company.

There was nothing horrid in all the world then—no illness, pain, germs or stinging nettles—and Adam and Eve only knew how to be good and happy.

Everything could have stayed like that for ever, but God had a terrible enemy—Satan. Once he had been a beautiful angel, but he had become proud and wicked, so God had to throw him out of heaven. Satan hated God so much that he was furious when he saw how God was enjoying his new friends.

"If only I could make them do something bad," he thought, "it would spoil all God's plans." Then he had an idea. God had only made one rule.

"You can have anything in the world that you want," God told Adam and Eve, "except the fruit of the tree in the middle of the garden."

God knew if they ate THAT fruit they would know about bad things as well as good, and he wanted to keep them safe from everything that was horrid.

One day, when Eve was sitting alone, Satan pretended to be a snake and he slithered up to her and hissed, "The fruit on the middle tree looks gorgeous. Are you QUITE sure God said you couldn't eat it?"

"Oh yes," replied Eve, "we mustn't even touch it, or one day we will die."

"But that's not true," lied Satan. "Go on, you try some."

Eve stood gazing up at the tree. Perhaps she should believe Satan? Slowly she reached out her hand and the next minute she was crunching her teeth into the sweet, juicy fruit.

"Adam, Adam!" she shouted. "Try some of this, it's lovely."

When God came into the garden that evening, Adam and Eve were hiding. They knew what a dreadful thing they had done, and because their hearts had turned bad they began to blame each other and the snake—but they wouldn't say sorry. Satan had used them to bring into the world everything that makes us unhappy.

God knew at once what had happened and he was desperately sad. "You will have to leave this garden," he said, "and work hard for your food, because now the weeds will grow and the insects will eat your plants. Pain and illness will spoil your lives and one day you will die."

God had warned them—but how sad he was as he watched them walk out of the garden. Satan thought he had won, but God was already making a secret plan to save people from death.

THE QUARRELING BROTHERS

BROTHERS DON'T ALWAYS like each other, and two of Adam and Eve's sons were always fighting. The trouble was, they were both so different. Cain spent all his time growing things to eat, like corn and vegetables, while Abel made friends with the sheep and goats. He loved looking after them, finding them juicy grass to eat and protecting them from other animals which had grown wild and fierce.

"It's not fair, Abel!" Cain would bellow. "I have to work away struggling with these wretched weeds and insects all day, while all you do is wander round with those silly sheep, talking to God all the time."

That was the real reason why Cain was so angry. Abel loved God and was his friend, while Cain didn't want to know God at all.

At night Abel used to stay out on the hills with his flocks, listening for bears or lions who might hurt them. He was never lonely since God was always close to him.

"I'd like to give God a present," he thought one night, "to show how much I love him." But he didn't have anything to give, except his animals, so he chose his prettiest lamb and gave that to God.

When Cain realized how pleased God was with Abel, he was jealous. "I'd better give God a present as well," he thought

crossly, and he collected a few of his vegetables. But God knew Cain was not his friend really, so he did not accept his present.

That made Cain furious. He sat in his field watching his brother and planning ways to hurt Abel. "I hate him!" he thought angrily.

"Be careful, Cain," warned the voice of God. "Satan wants you in his power, so he'll try and make you do something terrible." But Cain would not listen to God.

"Come for a walk, Abel," he called, "it's time we became friends." But as soon as Cain thought no one was looking, he picked up the sharp stone he used for digging and hit Abel so hard that he died. Then quickly he buried his brother deep in the ground.

Just as he was walking home God's voice made him jump with fright. "Where is your brother?"

"I don't know," lied Cain. "I don't have to look after him all the time." But God knew what he had done.

"Cain," he said, "you will have to go away from your home and your farm and spend the rest of your life wandering around the world. I saw what you did to Abel."

Once again God was very sad, and Adam and Eve missed their two sons. How they must have wished they had never eaten that fruit.

A BOAT FULL OF ANIMALS

THE WHOLE WORLD was in a horrible mess, and God was sorry he had ever made people. It was hundreds of years since Adam and Eve had lived, and people had spread out all over the earth. They did not love God or want to know him; they hated one another too, and spent their lives killing and stealing.

"I just cannot let this go on," thought God sadly. "Noah and his family are the only good people. I shall have to punish everyone else."

"Noah," said God one day, "I am going to flood the whole earth. Build a huge boat, with enough room for your family and some of every kind of animal, bird and insect, as well as all the food you will need for a year."

"That WILL have to be a big boat," thought Noah, and began cutting down trees for wood.

"Whatever are you doing now, Noah?" jeered the bad people. How they laughed when Noah said he was making a boat. "But we're miles from the sea," they giggled. "You're crazy!"

"Unless you tell God you're sorry for the bad things you do," said Noah quietly, "you're all going to be drowned." But no one believed him.

It took Noah and his three sons ages and ages to finish their boat and then to collect all the different kinds of creatures. How everyone laughed as they watched them trying to push all those animals up the gangplank!

But then it began to rain. "Perhaps Noah was right after all!" they wailed as they splashed about in the puddles and started to get very wet indeed.

The rain swelled the streams and sent them surging into the sea. The tide rose higher and higher and huge waves swept inland—and still it rained! The people climbed trees, hills and mountains, but the water rose up and covered them all, while Noah's boat rocked safely on the waves until the rain finally stopped.

What a noise there must have been inside that boat—barking, squawking, mooing, roaring and croaking! And think of the smell! Noah and his family had to live with that for months, but they were so pleased to be alive they didn't mind at all.

But one day, quite suddenly, they all felt a great bump; the boat had stuck on top of a mountain. "The flood must be going down at last," said Noah.

It took the wind and the sun many more weeks to dry up all the oozy, black mud that covered everything. Then one day, when Noah set free a little, grey dove, she came back with some fresh leaves in her beak. "Plants are beginning to grow again," smiled Noah. "It won't be long now before there is enough food for the animals."

And sure enough, a day finally came when they were able to open up the boat and let the creatures run, hop, fly or wiggle away to freedom.

Suddenly as the family stood by their great stranded boat, the whole sky was lit by a rainbow. "I promise never again to drown the world," said the voice of God, "and this rainbow is my sign to you that I shall keep my word."

THE MAN WHO LOST EVERYTHING

ONE DAY SATAN went to see God. He was feeling very pleased with himself. People were living all over the earth again, but not many of them loved God.

"But I do have one special friend," said God. "Have you noticed Job?" Satan's nasty smile slipped a bit. "He is the kindest man on earth," continued God.

"Yes, but he's also the richest," sneered Satan. "He's your favorite; you give him everything. Look at all those sheep, camels and donkeys! He's only your friend for what he gets out of it. Take everything away from him and he'll soon hate you."

"No he wouldn't!" said God. "He loves me for myself, not for what I give to him."

"Let me prove it," sneered Satan.

"Right," replied God, "but you mustn't hurt Job himself."

Not long afterwards Job was sitting in his fine house when one of his men banged on the door. "There's been a dreadful thunderstorm," the man exclaimed. "All your sheep and the other shepherds have been killed."

Before he had finished speaking another farm worker rushed in. "Enemy soldiers have killed the other men and taken away the camels and donkeys," he cried.

In those days people used animals and servants as money; there were no coins and dollar bills. Poor Job! Suddenly he had nothing left.

"Terrible news!" shouted another man as he ran up. "Your ten children were at a party when a great wind blew the house down and killed them all!"

Job got up and ripped his clothes into little pieces to show how sad he was. "God gave me everything and now he has taken it all away, but I still love him," was all he said.

When he heard that, Satan was very cross. "He's still a strong man," he said to God. "But if you let me make him ill and if he then loses all his friends, he'd be really angry with you."

Soon poor Job was terribly ill and covered with horrible spots and sore places.

"Get him out of the city," shouted everyone. "We might catch it too!" So Job was driven out of the city to sit on the rubbish heap all alone. Even his wife turned against him.

"You must have done something terribly bad for God to let all this happen to you," said people who used to be his friends.

Job could not understand God. For months he was ill and everyone was mean to him, but even though he was terribly miserable he still went on trusting God.

Finally God just could not keep quiet any longer and he told everyone in a loud voice just how angry he was with them all. After Job had prayed for them he was made well again, and God gave him twice as much as he ever had before.

Job had ten more children and lived a long and happy life with his family.

THE GREAT PLAN

YOU CAN'T SEE GOD, so how do you know he's there?" That's what people were always saying to God's friend Abraham. God was very sad when they made up their own pretend gods modeled out of gold or stone.

"I want you to leave this city," he said to Abraham one day. Abraham was rather startled. He loved the luxurious city of Ur and he had many friends there.

"Far away there lies a beautiful land called Canaan," continued God. "I want to give it to you and your children."

"Why?" asked Abraham.

"Because no one knows what I am really like except you. I want your family to be my own special people so I can show the rest of the world that I am loving and kind by the way I look after you."

"But my wife and I don't have any children," replied Abraham, feeling rather puzzled, "and we are far too old to start a family now."

"Abraham," replied God, "I have chosen you to be part of my secret plan. Will you trust me?"

"Yes," smiled Abraham, and hurried off to do his packing.

"You're mad!" gasped his friends. "Starting out on a journey when you don't even know where you're going, following a God you can't even SEE! Think of all the

robbers and wild animals you might meet, and you'll hate leaving your comfortable house for a drafty tent."

Abraham only smiled as he disappeared into the distance followed by his many servants and animals.

After many miles of dusty, dangerous traveling, they reached the land of Canaan, and Abraham and his wife Sarah settled down to wait for the family God had promised them.

But no baby came. Many years dragged by, and they grew even older.

"God's forgotten his promise," thought Sarah sadly, as she looked out of her tent one day. "It's far too late now."

Just then she saw three men trudging towards the camp. "They look tired," she thought kindly.

"Come in and have a meal," called Abraham, when he too saw the travelers.

What a good thing they did not let those men walk on in the scorching sun, because one of them was God, disguised as a man, and the other two were angels. Of course Abraham and Sarah did not know that as they hurried around getting the food ready.

When the visitors began to eat, Sarah peeped at them curiously from behind a curtain, and how surprised she was when she heard what they were saying to Abraham: "In nine months' time Sarah will have a baby son."

"That's impossible!" laughed Sarah to herself. "Abraham is nearly a hundred years old!" She had made no sound, but of course God knew just what she was thinking. "Why did Sarah laugh?" he asked. "Is anything too hard for God?"

Suddenly Sarah and Abraham realized just who their visitors really were. Nine months later they had a baby boy called Isaac, who became a very special part of God's plan.

HOW MUCH DO YOU LOVE ME?

ABRAHAM WAS very rich. He had so many animals and servants he could hardly count them. But his son Isaac was more precious to him than anything else. "How tall the boy is growing," thought the old man proudly, "and he is always laughing and kind. He's just right for God's plan."

But God was feeling sad as he watched Abraham sitting happily in the sun, because he knew he had to ask the old man to do a terribly difficult thing. God's plan could only work if Abraham trusted him completely, and God had to find out if he did.

"Abraham," said God in a voice that only his old friend could hear. "I want you to offer me a sacrifice." Abraham was pleased. He loved showing God how much he loved him by giving him a present of one of his animals. That is what a sacrifice meant.

"I want you to go to a hill a long way from here," continued God. "I don't want a sheep or a cow; this time I want your only son Isaac, whom you love so much." Poor Abraham was stunned. To offer Isaac as a sacrifice would mean he would have to burn him in a fire. How could God possibly want him to do that to Isaac?

"God knows what he's doing," Abraham told himself, but the very idea of hurting and frightening his son was terrible.

Very early next morning Abraham and Isaac set out on their long journey. God took them to the very hill where many years later he had to watch his own Son Jesus die as a sacrifice.

"Father," said Isaac, as they scrambled up the steep path, "I'm carrying the wood and you've got the pan of burning coals, but we've forgotten the lamb, haven't we?" Abraham must have felt like crying, but he managed to say, "God will provide the sacrifice, my son."

Together, out of the stones that lay about on top of the hill, they built a table and laid the wood ready. Then the dreadful moment came. Abraham took some rope and, tying Isaac up, he lifted him on to the table.

Now Isaac was a strong boy and Abraham was a very old man. Isaac could easily have struggled and run away, but he trusted his father, just like Abraham trusted God. So he made no sound. Abraham's hand was trembling as he lifted his sharp knife, and Isaac must have closed his eyes.

"Stop!" Just in time God's voice boomed across the silent afternoon.

"Don't hurt the boy, because now I know you love me more than anything else in the world."

Sighing with relief Abraham looked around and saw a ram caught by its horns in some brambles, so he offered that to God instead of Isaac.

As they sat close together by the embers of the fire they watched the stars appear in the night sky. Millions of them.

"I will make your family number as many as those stars," said God's voice. "And one day someone will be born into your family who will bless the whole world." God had actually told them the most important part of his secret plan.

THE TWINS

TWINS! How lovely!" Isaac had grown up and married a girl called Rebekah. They, like Abraham and Sarah, had also waited years for a baby, but suddenly God told them they were going to have two boys at once!

Before the twins were born, God said something very strange to their mother, Rebekah: "Remember, I have chosen the younger son to be part of my plan."

In those days it was always the oldest son of a chief who was given all the money and became head of the tribe. Esau was born first and he was a big, strong baby with a very loud voice. A few minutes later, Jacob followed him. He was much smaller and always very quiet and gentle.

As Isaac watched the boys grow up, he was puzzled. Esau, the older boy, seemed a far better kind of person for God's plan. "He is so strong and brave," thought Isaac. "Surely God should choose a boy like that and not little Jacob who's no good at games or hunting wild animals."

But God had not made a mistake. He knew that Esau did not care about him at

all, whereas Jacob loved God with all of his heart.

"It's just not fair!" thought Jacob. "If I had been born a few minutes before my brother, all God's promises and blessings would have been mine. I wish I were big and strong like Esau; then my father would love me too."

One day Jacob was cooking bean soup when Esau came staggering home tired out after a long hunting trip. "That smells delicious!" he said. "Give me some, I'm starving!"

"You can have it all, if you'll promise to let me be head of the tribe one day," said Jacob quickly. Esau promised at once, then gobbled up the soup. He couldn't care less.

Isaac grew old and blind, and, without asking God first, he said to Esau, "I want you to have everything when I die, so tonight I'm going to give you my last blessing to show everyone that you are to be head of the tribe. Now go into the hills and shoot a deer. Then you can cook me my favorite supper before I bless you."

When Rebekah and Jacob heard about this they were horrified. "Esau's forgotten the promise he made to me!" said Jacob. "And his father's forgotten the promise God made before you were born," added Rebekah.

Of course they should have talked to God at once, but instead they decided to do a very silly thing.

Genesis 27:6-45;   28:10-19

FRIGHTENED
IN THE NIGHT

YOU'RE GOING to dress up as your brother," said Rebekah to her favorite son Jacob. " We'll have to trick your father into giving you the blessing. Tonight I'll cook a delicious stew, and you can take it to him and pretend to be Esau."

"Father may be blind," protested Jacob, "but when he blesses me he'll FEEL I'm not all hairy like Esau."

Quickly Rebekah sewed goatskins round Jacob. "Put on your brother's clothes," she added, "so you smell like him too."

"Who's there?" quavered the old man, as Jacob sidled nervously into the tent.

"It's Esau, your oldest son," he lied, trying to make his voice sound gruff. The old man was puzzled.

"Come nearer," he said as he ran his shaky old hands over the goatskins. "You certainly feel and smell like Esau, but you sound like Jacob." But as he sniffed his favorite supper he soon forgot his suspicions.

When he had eaten an enormous meal he was so sleepy he gave his last blessing to the son he had never loved.

"I'll kill him!" The terrible, angry roar split the silence of the camp. Esau had come home and found that he had been

cheated by his brother. There was no way
that the promise could be changed.

"You must run away, Jacob," cried
Rebekah. "Go and stay with your uncle
Laban. He lives so far away, Esau will never
find you there."

All day long Jacob ran, and all the time
he kept looking nervously over his shoulder.
He was terrified Esau would chase him, so
he took the lonely path through the hills.
When darkness came, however, he was even
more frightened of the wild animals that
prowled among the rocks.

"I wish I were safely back at home!"
he thought as he lay down on the hard
ground and listened to the wind moaning
in the trees. How SAD he was that he had
told those lies. "Now I've lost everything,"
he thought, "and I'm all alone."

But he was wrong there! Because he
was sorry, God could forgive him and look
after him.

When at last he fell asleep with his head
on a flat stone, God sent him a wonderful
dream. A great staircase seemed to stretch
right up into heaven, and angels walked
up and down it all night long. Then, out of
the golden light of heaven, God actually
spoke to Jacob and told him he could still
be part of the great plan.

As soon as he woke up, Jacob thought,
"I must be special after all, because God
loves me, even if my father never did."

He was so grateful he wanted to give
God a present, but all he had was a little jar
of oil his mother had given him to rub on
cuts and blisters. So he poured it out over
the stone that had been his pillow. "I'll
come back to this place some day," he said.
"I'll call it Bethel, because I met God here."

As he walked off down the path to the
strange, far–off land, he felt like quite a
different person inside—because God had
told him he was not alone any more.

THE HORRIBLE UNCLE

JACOB DID NOT like his uncle Laban at all. He was such a nasty, greedy man. "Why not stay here with us?" Laban suggested, thinking that he could make his nephew work hard on the farm. Jacob was very happy to do that, because Laban had a beautiful daughter called Rachel. "I must be falling in love," he thought as he helped her with the sheep.

After a month Jacob had worked so hard that his uncle said, "I will give you anything, if only you will stay with us."

"I don't want wages," said Jacob, looking at Rachel over the supper table. "I'll work for seven years if you'll let me marry your daughter."

"Done!" said Laban with a glint in his mean, little eyes.

Rachel and Jacob loved each other so much that it seemed no time until their wedding day arrived. Then a dreadful thing happened. Laban dressed Rachel's plain sister Leah in the bride's veil, and married her to Jacob instead.

"He's so useful to me," cackled the horrid old uncle, "I'll make him work another seven years for the girl he really loves."

When Jacob found out he was furious. Now he understood what it felt like to be cheated.

"In this country," soothed Laban, "you can have as many wives as you like. Marry Rachel next week, but you'll have to work for her."

Life after that was not very happy for Jacob. Laban sat about, getting fat with the money Jacob worked so hard to earn for him, and the two sisters were always quarreling. Leah had many fine sons, but Rachel had to wait for years for a baby.

When at last her little boy Joseph was born, Jacob whispered, "This is the child who will be part of God's plan. We can go home now."

But when Laban heard that, he was horrified. "You can't go away," he said. "You haven't any money."

"I'll go on working for you," replied Jacob, "if you'll give me all the black-spotted sheep."

"Done!" said Laban happily, because most of his sheep were white!

That night God told Jacob a secret way to make white sheep have black-spotted lambs, and soon Jacob had a far bigger flock than Laban and he became very rich.

Laban was furious, and poor Jacob was so scared of him he decided to run away.

Secretly he loaded his wives and children on to camels and set off with all his servants and thousands of spotted sheep.

When Laban found out, he was livid and started out with all his men to chase them. "I'll make them sorry they left me," he muttered dangerously.

"I'm watching you!" warned God suddenly. "You are not to touch Jacob; he's my friend."

Laban was so frightened of God he had to slink back home and do his own farm work.

"God DID look after us well," said Jacob with a sigh of relief as they watched the horrid old uncle disappear in the distance. "I only hope he will protect us from my brother Esau as well. Come on everyone; let's go home to the land of Canaan."

THE DARK HOLE

THIS IS THE PLACE! Here's Bethel! Gather round everyone!" How excited Jacob was. They had been traveling for hundreds of miles, and after many adventures they were here at last.

"Those are the rocks where I heard the lions prowling, Joseph," he explained to his smallest son. "All I had then was a stick and a little jar of oil. Now just look at all God has given me!" Jacob smiled around at his big family and the crowds of servants and animals.

Even when Esau had marched to meet him with four hundred men, God had helped them become friends again. "I really thought he'd kill us all," shivered Jacob. "But Esau is so rich himself now, he doesn't mind about me being head of the tribe after our father Isaac. That's what you will be too, one day, Joseph," he added, smiling down at his favorite son, who must have been just about seven. "Everything will be lovely now we're home." But he was wrong.

When they reached a place that was later called Bethlehem, Rachel died. Poor Joseph! How he missed his mother, but she had left him a present, a new baby brother called Benjamin. "I won't let the other boys hurt you," whispered Joseph as he carried little Benjamin about on his back.

The ten big sons of Leah were always doing horrid things to Joseph. They hated him because his father loved him best and had given him a special colored coat to show that he would be the chief one day. "It's not fair," they growled. "Reuben's the oldest." So they began to make plans to kill Joseph.

One day, when the older boys were away looking after the sheep in a distant valley, Joseph's father said, "Your brothers have been gone so long, you go and see if they're all right."

Joseph knew it would not be safe for him to go alone, because they hated him, but he didn't like to tell tales to his father.

Joseph was still a long way off when they saw him coming. "Here's our chance," they whispered. "Let's throw him into that dark hole; he'll soon die down there."

"Let me out! Let me out!" screamed poor Joseph, but his horrid brothers only laughed as they sat down to their supper.

Just then some traders came riding by on their way to the rich land of Egypt.

"Would you like to buy a slave boy?" shouted Judah, and with a mean smile he whispered to his brothers, "Let's make some money as well as getting rid of Joseph for ever."

When a rope was dangled down into the darkness, Joseph thought he was being rescued. Instead he was tied to the back of a camel, and his brothers were each paid two silver pieces.

Joseph just could not help crying. "Will I ever see my father and little Benjamin again?" he wondered. "But God was with my father when he went off to a strange land, and I know he'll stay with me as well."

"Look!" said Jacob's ten sons, as they showed him the colored coat which they had covered in blood. "A wild animal must have eaten Joseph."

Poor Jacob was terribly sad, but God's plans had not really gone wrong.

THE DUNGEONS

IT WAS HORRIBLE waiting to be sold in a shop full of other slaves in the strange land of Egypt. Joseph made himself stand up straight and kept reminding himself that he was special because God loved him. He actually managed to look so brave that he was bought by Potiphar, the captain of the king's guard, and taken back to his grand house.

Joseph worked terribly hard there, because he wanted to please God, and soon Potiphar made him the head slave. Everything went well for Joseph until Potiphar's wife lost her temper with him one day and had him thrown into prison.

It was dark and damp in the dungeons and few prisoners ever came out alive. "But I can still work for God down here," he thought as he began to care for all the other prisoners.

One night a man had a dream which terrified him. "Help me, Joseph," he gasped. "Ask your God what this dream means."

"Don't be frightened," said Joseph when he had prayed. "The dream means you will soon be out of prison and back at work."

"My job is to pour the king's wine for him," smiled the man. "When I get back to the palace I'll ask him to set you free." But he soon forgot poor Joseph.

One night King Pharaoh had a terrible dream. "TELL ME WHAT IT MEANS!" he roared at everyone.

No one was clever enough to do that, so the king became dangerously angry. As the steward dashed round trying to soothe him with goblets of wine, he suddenly remembered Joseph. "Your Majesty," he gasped. "I DO know someone who could help you; how awful of me to forget!"

Soon soldiers were rushing to the dungeons down below.

"You can't go near the king looking like that!" they said in disgust when they saw Joseph's prison rags. "And just look at your hair and beard!" No one was ever cleaned up so quickly and soon Joseph was standing before Pharaoh himself.

"They tell me you understand dreams," said the king.

"No, Your Majesty, I don't," replied Joseph quietly, "but God does." Pharaoh looked down at Joseph for a long time. This slave was more like a prince than a prisoner.

"Seven fat cows came out of the River Nile," said Pharaoh. "Then seven terribly thin cows ate them all up, but they didn't get any fatter—whatever do you think that means?"

"Your Majesty," began Joseph, "God is warning you about dreadful things that are going to happen. Unless you do something quickly, all your people will die. For seven years so much corn will grow in Egypt that people will just throw it away. After that, seven terrible years will follow when nothing will grow at all. You must build great barns and save all that corn now, or thousands of animals and people will starve in the bad years."

"You are the cleverest man I know!" shouted the king. "You must tell everyone in Egypt what to do."

So, from being a ragged slave in a dungeon, Joseph became one of the most powerful men in the world. Which was JUST what God had planned.

THE PRIME MINISTER

EVERYONE ELSE in the world was hungry, but in Egypt there was plenty to eat, because Joseph shared fairly the corn he had saved in his great barns. When he heard that people in other lands were dying of hunger, he often worried about his father and Benjamin.

One day he had a terrible shock. His ten brothers arrived at the palace. "Send those men to me," he ordered his servants.

Were they still just as bad, he wondered, as he sat on his golden throne. He looked so grand in all his robes his brothers did not know him, so he decided to find out if they had changed. "You're not from this land," he shouted, pretending to be angry. "You must be enemy spies."

"No, no, sir!" protested Judah. "We are here to buy food for our old father and young brother who are starving at home."

Would they sell Benjamin as a slave too, wondered Joseph. "Bring your brother to me," he roared, "or you shall have no more food."

"We can't do that," protested Judah miserably. "If anything should happen to him our poor father would die."

"And would you care?" thought Joseph, as he remembered how cruel they had once been to him. "If you do not bring me your brother, I shall know you are spies!" he thundered.

"All this has happened because we did such a terrible thing to poor Joseph," they muttered nervously as they hurried home.

"All the Egyptian corn has been eaten now, Father," said Judah a few months later.

"Unless we take Benjamin back there with us, we are all going to die."

"But he's all I've got left," sobbed Jacob.

"I will guard him with my life," promised Judah.

When Joseph saw them all waiting in his palace one day, it was hard not to hug Benjamin, but he had to stick to his plan. He sent them off with bulging sacks of corn and they still never guessed who he was.

They were riding away sighing with relief when something dreadful happened.

"Stop!" shouted one of Joseph's servants, as he came riding after them. "One of you must have stolen my master's best silver cup. The thief will be his slave for ever."

When all the corn sacks were searched, the missing goblet was found in Benjamin's bag, just where Joseph had secretly put it.

"The rest of you can go home," said the servant, "but this boy comes with me." As he began to drag poor Benjamin back towards the city, the ten brothers began to cry. "We can't leave him," they said. "We'll all go back."

"Please sir," said Judah as he knelt once again before Joseph, "let me be your slave instead of Benjamin. We would all rather die than see our father sad again."

At last Joseph knew they were different, so he told them who he was. "God planned this," he told them. "He knew you would all die of hunger unless I saved the corn. Go back home and fetch Father and the rest of the tribe; then come back here and live with me in Egypt so I can look after you all."

THE BABY
IN THE BASKET

IT WAS MANY hundreds of years after Joseph had saved Egypt from famine. Jacob and his sons were dead, but they had had so many great-great- grandchildren that there were millions of them living in Egypt now, and they were called Jews.

A new Pharaoh came to rule the land, who had never heard of Joseph. One day he was floating down the River Nile in his brightly painted boat. "There are far too many of these Jews," he snarled. "They're living on the best land in my kingdom. Just look at all their fat sheep eating my grass! I'll have to get rid of them. They might fight against us Egyptians one day, and anyway I want to use their land for building."

"You shall be our slaves!" he shouted angrily across the water. "You'll work so hard you'll soon die."

Day after day, in the blistering sun, the poor Jews were bullied by Egyptians with great whips. They hardly had any food as they were forced to build cities, palaces and pyramids.

"There are still too many of them," muttered Pharaoh. "Soldiers," he ordered, "every time a Jewish baby boy is born, throw it into the river!"

"Oh God, help us!" cried the poor Jews, and God heard them. One day in a little slave hut, a very special baby was born.

"We can't let him be drowned," sobbed his mother, "but if we keep him here the soldiers are bound to hear him cry."

So they made a floating cradle for Moses, out of a waterproof basket. In the morning, long before anyone was awake, they crept down to the river and hid the basket amongst the reeds. Miriam, the baby's big sister, was left on guard.

The gentle lapping of the water soon rocked Moses to sleep, and Miriam began to weave a mat of reeds. Then, suddenly, she was stiff with fear. Someone was coming. Down the path from the palace came the princess, Pharaoh's own daughter. Poor Miriam was shaking with fright as she watched the princess slide into the water for a swim.

"Wade over and get me that funny little basket," said the princess to one of her maids, and Miriam closed her eyes in horror.

"Oh look!" exclaimed the princess. "It's a darling little Jewish baby. I won't let father drown him; he shall be mine for always."

Just at that moment Moses began to cry loudly. "Oh dear!" said the princess doubtfully. "He's probably hungry."

Quickly Miriam slipped out of her hiding place and said, "Would you like me to find someone to look after your baby for you?"

"Thank you," said the princess. She was pleased to find someone to feed the baby.

Of course Miriam ran straight to fetch her mother, who looked after Moses until he moved to the royal palace. She told him the secret about the beautiful land God had promised to give his family one day. "You must grow up to be a clever and powerful prince, my son," she would whisper. "Then perhaps you can save your people from being slaves and take them back to their own land."

33

THE RUNAWAY PRINCE

PRINCE MOSES rode along proudly in his chariot. He was on his way to see how the Jewish slaves were being treated. Moses liked being a prince. He rode fast horses, wore fine clothes and ate nice food. He had done very well at school and everyone knew he was brave, powerful and clever.

"I am ready now to help my people," he thought, but he was so proud of himself he forgot to ask God what he should do.

As his fine chariot swished through the muddy building site he was horrified when he saw the poor, thin slaves. One old man was so tired he just could not carry his load of heavy bricks and he crumpled to the

ground. Moses was furious when he saw a cruel Egyptian beating him with a whip. No one seemed to be looking, so he jumped down from his chariot, pulled a dagger from his belt and killed the man.

"Now my people will know I have come to save them," he thought grandly as he pushed the Egyptian into a hole and covered him with sand. But he was wrong.

"Who told you to be our leader?" said the slaves, and one of them, who had seen what Moses had done, went and told King Pharaoh.

"He shall die!" shouted Pharaoh in a rage.

It was years later, and Moses was an old man now. He had been so frightened of Pharaoh he had run away to hide in a lonely place called a desert. There was nothing there but sand and rocks, and the proud prince had become a poor shepherd.

But a wonderful thing happened. As he wandered around, looking for patches of dry grass to feed his sheep, he had learned to know and love God.

"I am actually happy here," he thought one day. "But I do hope Miriam and my brother Aaron are all right in Egypt. I never did anything to help the slaves after all."

Suddenly he saw a strange fire burning on Sinai, the highest mountain in the desert. As he walked towards it a deep voice spoke to him from the centre of the flames.

"Moses!"

"Who's there?" gasped Moses nervously.

"I am God," came the voice again. "I have seen how cruelly my people are treated in Egypt and I have heard their cry for help. Go and tell the king to set them free."

"ME?" exclaimed Moses in horror. "But I'm only an old shepherd. The king won't listen to me."

"I will make him," said God. "Then you can take the slaves back to the land I always promised them."

"But I've lived alone so long I've forgotten how to talk to people," protested Moses.

"I will tell you what to say," said God, "and I have told your brother Aaron to help you. Even now he is on his way here to find you."

So Moses stopped arguing and, calling his sheep, he began the long walk back to Egypt.

TOO MANY FROGS

"WHAT WAS THAT?" bellowed Pharaoh as he glared down from his throne at Moses and Aaron.

"The Lord God says, 'Let my people go', " they repeated.

"Who IS this Lord God?" scoffed Pharaoh. "I've never heard of him. And if I let the slaves go, who would do all the work? You are lazy! From now on you'll do twice as much and I'll have you beaten even harder."

Soon the poor Jews were so tired and frightened they did not want to think about God or the land he promised.

"What went wrong, Lord?" prayed Moses in despair.

"What I am about to do," said God, "will show everyone just how powerful I really am. Go down to the River Nile early in the morning when Pharaoh has his swim and tell him that terrible things will happen in Egypt until he lets my people go."

"Bah!" mocked Pharaoh, but as soon as he put his toes into the river he realized God had changed the water into thick, red blood. No one in Egypt had anything to drink for days and all the fish died and smelled terrible.

Then God sent millions of frogs. They jumped into Pharaoh's bed and tickled him; they hopped about the table at dinner time and fell into his soup. No one could walk a step without falling over frogs.

"Moses!" yelled Pharaoh. "Tell God to take these frogs away and the people can go." But as soon as the frogs were gone he changed his mind.

Then in flew clouds of stinging flies and they bit the Egyptians all over. Pharaoh scratched until he bled, and when all his farm animals died he was furious, but he wouldn't change his mind.

After that came thunderstorms. The hailstones were so big they broke the trees and crashed through the roofs of houses. Pharaoh was simply terrified of lightning. "I'm sorry I've been so bad," he squeaked at Moses from under the table in his palace. "Please ask God to stop this storm and the slaves can go."

"When I pray, it will stop," replied Moses. "Then you will know the whole earth belongs to the Lord." But when the thunder died away Pharaoh changed his mind again.

So along came swarms of insects called locusts. They ate up all the plants, leaves and grass and left Egypt like a desert.

Into the palace crowded all the most important people. "Let the Jews go!" they pleaded. "Don't you realize there's nothing left to eat? We're ruined!"

As soon as Pharaoh asked Moses to pray, God sent a wind to blow away the locusts. Then Pharaoh muttered, "Good! Now the slaves will stay."

God was now very angry with Pharaoh, so he stopped the sun from shining and made it night all the time. Pharaoh and all the Egyptians were petrified of the dark, as they groped about bumping into each other.

"This time the slaves really can go," shrieked Pharaoh, but as soon as the sun shone again he forgot his promise.

"BE VERY CAREFUL, Pharaoh," warned Moses angrily, "or God will have to do something so dreadful that everyone in Egypt will be crying."

"Bah!" shrugged Pharaoh and turned his back on Moses.

BLOOD ON THE DOOR

HURRY UP, pack everything. We're leaving!" Moses and Aaron told the slaves.

"But Pharaoh hasn't said we can go," they replied nervously.

"By tomorrow morning," said Moses sadly, "he will be begging us to leave. Tonight God will move through the land and the oldest son in every family will die."

"What about our boys?" gasped the slaves.

"God will keep your children safe, but this is what you must do. Every family is to choose their best lamb and kill it in the evening, then paint their door posts with the blood. When God sees that red blood, he will pass over your houses."

So many terrible things had been happening that the Egyptians were really frightened by this time. They knew God was more powerful than Pharaoh and longed for the king to let the slaves go free. So they were glad as they watched the slaves scurrying about packing all their things. "They're going at last," they said. "Let's give them a present of our jewels and best clothes."

That night the slaves ate as much supper as they could manage, but they ate it standing up with their walking shoes on and their bundles in their hands. The oldest boy in every family must have been very worried. "Are you SURE God will pass over our house?" they kept asking.

"Of course," replied their fathers, "the lamb died instead of you."

When it was deadly quiet in the middle of the night, a terrible scream came from the palace. Pharaoh had found his oldest son the prince was dead. "Why didn't I listen to Moses?" he wailed. Soon people in every house in Egypt were crying for their sons too.

"GO!" shouted Pharaoh, long before it was morning, and out of all the tumbledown slave huts they came, striding off towards the promised land.

The fathers drove the sheep and goats along in little flocks. Grannies helped the little children, and mothers held the babies. Everyone else carried as much as they could manage wrapped up in blankets on their backs. They looked so grand wearing all the Egyptians' best things they did not feel like slaves any more.

That night each family put up a little tent and lit a camp fire to cook their supper, and as the children lay looking up at the stars they thought they had never been so happy in all their lives.

But unfortunately that happiness did not last long.

WALKING THROUGH THE SEA

HOWEVER ARE WE going to find the way to this land God's promised us?" someone asked Moses as they started off next morning.

"God won't let us get lost," replied Moses. " Look."

There in front of them was a huge cloud. It was more like the smoke from a great bonfire stretching up to the sky. It moved along in front of them as they walked, and stopped when it was time to rest. At night it glowed red like fire and gave light to everyone in the camp. No one was afraid of the dark any more.

After a few days the moving cloud led them to the seaside. The slave children had never been to the sea before and they had such fun paddling and making sand castles. Fathers and mothers sunbathed and the animals lay down to rest.

Then, suddenly, far in the distance behind them they heard a rumbling noise. Everyone jumped up in terror; they knew just what it was. Pharaoh had changed his mind yet again and he was coming after them with thousands of soldiers. Nearer and nearer they came, until the Jews could see the galloping war horses and the sun glinting on sharpened swords.

"We're trapped!" they cried. Before them lay the sea, high mountains rose on either side, and behind them was Pharaoh and all his army.

"You should never have brought us out of Egypt, Moses," sobbed the people as they dashed about, falling over each other in their panic.

"Stand still!" boomed Moses, "and let God fight the Egyptians for you." Suddenly everyone realized that the cloud had moved. It was behind them now, blocking the soldiers' view so they could not see where they were charging.

"God says, 'Go forward'!" shouted Moses as he held his shepherd's stick out over the waves.

"We can't march right into the sea!" protested the people. "We haven't any boats; we'll be drowned."

But then they saw what was happening. A terrific wind was blowing a path right through the sea for them. The water rose up in two great mountains on either side as they hurried through the gap to safety. It took all night for everyone to reach the other side, and by the time it was light Pharaoh had arrived on the beach.

"After them!" he shouted, and into the mud plunged his horses and chariots. The Egyptians were halfway across the sea when the last Jew arrived on the far shore. Down in the soft mud sank the wheels of the chariots and soon the horses' hooves were stuck as well. The soldiers began to feel frightened.

"Let's go back!" they shrieked, but they were too late. The waves came crashing back over their heads and soon the whole Egyptian army was lost.

"Now we know God has really set us free at last," said the slaves. "Pharaoh and his soldiers will never be cruel to us again."

Exodus 15, 16, 17

DANGER!

"WHY IS GOD taking us through this desert?" grumbled the people. "It's such a dangerous place, and there's not nearly enough food and water here for so many of us."

"God wants you to see how well he can look after you," replied Moses.

"But we've had no water for three days!" complained the people. "We shall die of thirst soon." Just then, someone noticed a little pool over the hill and they all began to run towards it, holding out their cups.

"Ugh! We can't drink this!" they shouted in disgust. "It tastes terrible." Even the animals spat out the nasty water and the children began to cry.

Angrily the fathers turned on Moses, but he was busy praying.

"There's a tree over there," said God. "If you cut it down and throw it into the pool, the water will taste good."

"There, you see!" said Moses as the people drank the fresh water. "God always looks after his people."

But the Jews still were not sure they could really trust God.

Deeper and deeper into the desert went the swirling cloud and day after day the people tramped along behind it. There were no shops, just sand and rocks, so they soon ran out of food.

"We're hungry," they muttered crossly. "Why did we ever leave Egypt?" The people never thought of asking God to help them, and that made him very sad. But when Moses prayed, God did something very special.

Early next morning the ground was covered in what looked like little, white seeds. They tasted delicious, like biscuits made of honey.

"Get up," cried Moses, "and collect as much as you need today." The little "seeds," called manna, were there every morning until they reached the land of Canaan.

Hunger and thirst, however, were not the only dangers of the desert. Behind the jagged rocks, fierce tribesmen were lurking. They did not like the Jews walking through their desert and they wanted the Egyptian jewels. Out they sprang and began to chop the people at the back of the line with their axes and swords.

Moses heard the terrible screams and looked back in alarm. "Quickly Joshua," he said to the bravest young man he knew, "choose some strong men and, while you fight, I will climb up that high mountain and ask God to help you."

The robbers were big and strong and good at fighting. Joshua and his men were not soldiers; they had been nothing but slaves all their lives. Yet they knew that high above them, on the mountain, Moses was praying, so they fought bravely. By the time the sun went down the robbers were beaten. All night long the people thanked God, for they knew he had won the battle for them.

43

THE RUMBLING MOUNTAIN

IT WAS THE HIGHEST mountain the Jews had ever seen. Out of the dry, flat desert it towered. Mount Sinai—it almost seemed to reach the sky.

"That is where God first spoke to me," Moses told them. "Now he wants to talk to all of you, here on Sinai."

But the people were terrified at the thought of hearing God speak, because they did not know him very well then. So as they stood around the bottom of the great mountain their teeth chattered with fright.

A great, dark cloud of smoke covered the peak of the mountain. Fire spurted out from among the rocks, which rumbled and shook. God's voice echoed around and around the silent desert and the people clutched each other with fear.

Yet God only wanted to tell them how much he loved them. "The whole earth belongs to me," he said, "but I have chosen you to be my special people, so that you can show everyone else what I am like."

He told them about the beautiful land he was giving to them and he gave them some rules to keep when they got there. No one is ever happy when they are doing bad things and God wanted them to be happy. So he told them they were not to kill people, tell lies or swear. They were to have a day of rest every week and be good to their mothers and fathers. They must not even want something that belonged to someone else and they were certainly never to steal it. Above all, God wanted them to love him and to know he loved them too. So they were NEVER, NEVER to make pretend gods like those they had seen in Egypt.

"Will you make a pact with me?" asked God. "I will promise to look after you and your children for ever if you will promise to love me and keep my rules."

"We promise," said all the people.

"If you break that promise," warned God, "expect trouble."

"We will never, never break our promise," they said.

How different everything would have been if they really had kept that promise.

Exodus 32; Deuteronomy 9; God's tent described in Exodus 25-31, 35-40

THE GOLDEN BULL

"I AM GOING BACK up the mountain alone," Moses told the people one day. "God wants to tell me how we should live in our new land. I shall write it all down in a book so we shall never forget it." Of course there was no paper in the desert, so Moses took some large, flat stones instead.

"Imagine daring to go up there alone," whispered the people. Day after day they gazed up at the mountain, but Moses did not come back.

"Perhaps he's dead," whispered someone. Soon they were all standing outside their tents in little nervous groups.

"Maybe God doesn't love us after all," they muttered. "Whatever will become of us, stuck out here alone in the desert?"

"We need a god we can see," someone shouted, "like they had in Egypt."

"Their gods were so pretty," everyone agreed, "all shiny gold and sparkling with jewels."

"We could make a god like that for ourselves out of the things the Egyptians gave us," someone suggested, and they all thought that was a marvelous idea. How soon they had forgotten their promise to God.

Soon they had made a huge, golden bull. "This will be our god now," they said, and began to dance round it, singing songs to it and giving it presents. How SAD God was when he saw them.

"Look!" shouted a voice, and suddenly the music died away and the dancers froze like statues. There, coming towards them down the mountain, was Moses—and he looked terribly angry.

"Whatever have you done?" he demanded in a dreadful voice, and, throwing the stone books to the ground, he smashed them into tiny pieces. "You have broken your promise to God already!" he boomed.

Savagely he ground the golden bull to dust, mixed it with water and made the people drink it all up. Many of them died that day and the rest huddled in their tents crying bitterly. Moses himself lay face downwards on the ground and did not move for days.

At first God was so sad and angry he wanted to destroy the people completely. But when Moses prayed, God was able to forgive them.

Sadly Moses went back up the mountain again with more flat stones. And when he came down he had wonderful news: "God wants us to make him a huge tent, a traveling church. We must start work at once."

It took them months to make that tent. But at last it was finished and they all stood and gazed in wonder. It must have been the biggest and most beautiful tent in the world. The most precious thing of all was the golden box, called the ark, where they kept the stone book Moses had written on the mountain—the very first Bible.

Suddenly, the dazzling, bright cloud that had led them from Egypt came and settled over the Lord's tent to show them that he was there.

"He does love us," whispered the people, "and now we can talk to him and give him presents whenever we like." And they all went happily back to their tents.

FRIGHTENED SPIES

THE CLOUD'S moving!" As the shout rang around the campsite, everyone dashed about packing up their tents. At last, after many months, they were leaving Mount Sinai.

The huge procession began to form up behind the cloud. First came the priests, Aaron's family, carrying the golden box they called the ark. It went in front of the people to remind them of the promise they had made to God and his promise to look after them.

Yet, as they all walked along behind it, they became more and more nervous. "There'll be people living there already," they whispered. "Suppose they fight us?"

When at last they reached the end of the desert, Moses shouted, "Look! There! Over the river lies the land God has given you. We will march in and enjoy it."

"Let's send some spies in first," suggested the people cautiously, "so they can tell us what the people are like."

"All right," shrugged Moses, and chose twelve young men. But only two of them, Joshua and his friend Caleb, really trusted God; the other ten men were secretly frightened inside.

"They're back!" shouted the Jews after weeks of waiting for the spies. "Tell us what the land was like," they added as they all clustered round.

"It's lovely!" began Joshua and Caleb, but the other ten men interrupted them. They were so frightened they made up lies which filled the Jews with terror.

"The people of Canaan are giants!" they began. "They are much stronger than we are, and they live in great towns surrounded by thick walls. Really, the land isn't such a good place after all. Perhaps we shouldn't bother to go there. How could there ever be enough food for all of us? We didn't see any crops growing."

"That's not true!" protested Joshua and Caleb. "Look at all this fruit we brought back. The people certainly ARE tall and strong, but God said he'd give us the land, so he will help us to fight them. Don't you remember what happened to Pharaoh and his army?"

But the people were so frightened they preferred to listen to the other spies and they began to throw stones at Joshua and Caleb.

"Moses told us lies!" they stormed. "We should never have listened to him and left Egypt. We'll find a new leader and go back there now."

If Moses had not quickly prayed for the Jews, God would certainly have destroyed them at once because he was so hurt and disappointed.

"None of these slaves will ever live in my promised land," he said. "They must go back into the desert for forty years until they all grow old and die. Then I will lead their children and grandchildren into Canaan. Only Joshua and Caleb will live long enough to see the land."

Before night all ten of the frightened spies were dead and the people went to the Lord's tent to say how sorry they were. But by then the cloud was moving them back into the desert again.

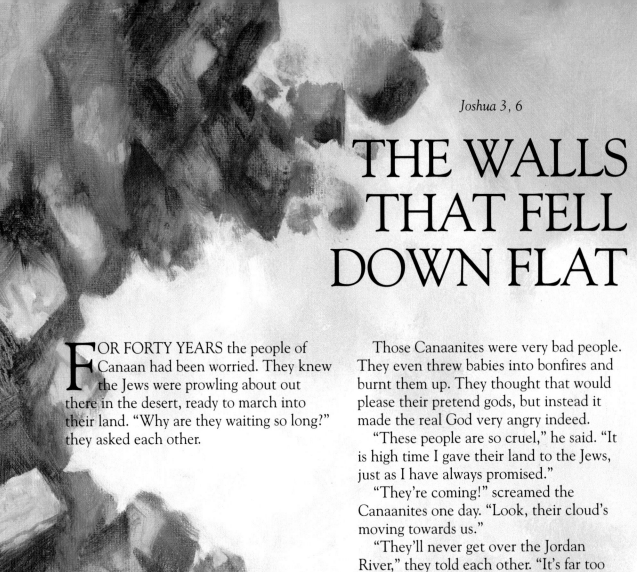

THE WALLS THAT FELL DOWN FLAT

FOR FORTY YEARS the people of Canaan had been worried. They knew the Jews were prowling about out there in the desert, ready to march into their land. "Why are they waiting so long?" they asked each other.

Those Canaanites were very bad people. They even threw babies into bonfires and burnt them up. They thought that would please their pretend gods, but instead it made the real God very angry indeed.

"These people are so cruel," he said. "It is high time I gave their land to the Jews, just as I have always promised."

"They're coming!" screamed the Canaanites one day. "Look, their cloud's moving towards us."

"They'll never get over the Jordan River," they told each other. "It's far too deep and wide."

But as they watched the priests carry the golden box into the water, the river stopped flowing and all the Jews walked over, just as God had told them to do.

"Run into Jericho!" shouted the Canaanites. "The walls of the city are so thick we'll be safe there."

As the huge, iron gates slammed shut, they felt much better, and when nothing happened for three days the Canaanites began to laugh!

"They're scared!" they said. But they were wrong. The Jews had learned to trust God in those forty long years in the desert and they were just waiting for him to tell them what to do next. Joshua was their leader now that Moses had died, and the people knew that God was with him.

Of course there was no way they could ever get into Jericho; those walls were far too strong. But God knew what to do.

Early one morning the Canaanites were woken up by a strange sound. "The Jews are marching around our city," they said, "carrying a golden box and blowing their trumpets."

Every day for a week the same thing happened and the Canaanites began to get nervous. "Whatever are they trying to do?" they whispered.

On the seventh day God told the Jews to march around Jericho, not once, but seven times. Then they had to make as much noise as they possibly could. As they shouted and blew their horns, the great city walls began to rattle and shake and enormous cracks appeared between the bricks. The Canaanites were horrified.

Then, with a terrible rumbling crash, the walls collapsed, all the way around the city. The people inside were much too frightened to fight, and all the Jews had to do was walk in and capture Jericho.

After many battles and great adventures the whole land was theirs, and Joshua gave everyone a little farm and a house of their very own. "This is lovely!" they said, as they looked at the green fields and juicy fruit.

Joshua told the priests to pitch God's tent on top of a high hill. Then he called everyone together and said: "God has been good to you. Now you are safely here, will you keep your promise to him?"

"Of course we will!" the people shouted.

"And you won't start worshiping pretend gods?" persisted Joshua.

"Never!" they all replied.

How happy they would all have been, if only they had kept that promise.

NIGHT ATTACK

GIDEON WAS the youngest in the family and he was always feeling frightened. Most people thought he was stupid because he loved God, whereas nearly everyone else preferred a pretend god called Baal. Ugly models of him were placed on the hills and under big trees all over the land.

It was many years since the people had made their promise to God. Now they had forgotten it, so He had stopped looking after them. Over the river from the desert came thousands of terrible thieves called Midianites. They rode on fast camels and swooped down on the little farms, stealing the animals and crops. Soon there was nothing left to eat and the people ran away and lived in caves.

Gideon was so terrified he hid under an oak tree.

One day, as he was crouching there, an angel spoke to him. "God is with you, brave man," he said. No one had ever called Gideon brave before! "God is sending you to drive all these Midianites out of his land," continued the angel.

"ME!" exclaimed Gideon in astonishment

"God will help you," replied the angel. God often seems to use weak, frightened people in his plan.

Soon everyone in the land was talking about Gideon and the angel. "We should

never have broken our promise to God," they said. "Baal can't really help us."

More and more Midianites poured across the Jordan River, and they set up a huge army camp in a deep valley.

Thousands of people crept out of their hiding places to join Gideon, but God told him to send most of them home. "I only want three hundred men," said God.

"But there are thousands of Midianites," protested Gideon nervously.

"I want everyone to know that I won this battle," replied God. "When it is dark, you and your three hundred men are to creep to the enemy camp and surround it. Every man must carry a burning torch hidden in a clay jar."

"That's a funny way to go into battle," Gideon's men must have thought. But God had already sent the Midianites such frightening dreams that they were all crouching in their tents scaring one another horribly.

Suddenly, from all around them they heard a terrifying crash. How they jumped! It was only Gideon's men breaking their clay pots on the stones, but it sounded like thousands of war horses.

As the Midianites wriggled out of their tents they saw lights springing up all over the hills above them. "We're surrounded," they gasped; they never realized it was only Gideon's three hundred torches. When his men began to shout, the noise echoed round and round the rocks, until the Midianites thought millions of soldiers were attacking them from all sides.

It was so dark they couldn't see who they were fighting, so they picked up their swords and started slashing out at each other. How Gideon and his men must have laughed as they chased them all home.

"They won't come back," smiled Gideon. "Now let's burn all those models of Baal."

The boy who was always frightened had become leader of all the people.

THE STRONG MAN

SAMSON WAS THE strongest man who had ever lived. God made him like that for a special reason.

The Jews had forgotten God again, and he was so angry with them he let terrible enemies come and rule the land. They were not just wandering thieves this time, but very fierce soldiers called Philistines.

"Oh God, we are sorry!" prayed the Jews and they threw away their models of Baal.

It was then that a very remarkable baby arrived.

"Before you were born," Samson's mother often told him, "God sent an angel to tell me that I must never, never cut your hair, to show everyone that you are very special."

Soon Samson was growing enormous and he was so strong he began terrifying the Philistines. He managed to set fire to all their crops and fruit trees. Soon their whole land was blazing and the Philistines had nothing left to eat.

They were wild with rage. So when Samson went into one of their walled cities to stay with a friend, they shut and locked the big, heavy gates. "We have him now!" they laughed.

But Samson got up in the night, wrenched open the gates and carried them up a hill thirty miles away!

"We must catch him," raged the Philistines and sent an army to look for him. The Jews were so frightened; they tied Samson's arms and legs and dragged him off to the enemy. But when Samson saw the Philistines he burst his ropes and ran towards them. He had no sword, but on the ground he saw a piece of bone from a donkey's jaw. Picking it up, he leapt into attack. He was so strong, a thousand Philistines were soon lying dead in heaps.

"We'll never catch him," fumed the Philistines; but in the end they did, and all because Samson was silly enough to fall in love with Delilah, a Philistine spy.

God had told his people only to marry other Jews, but Samson ignored God's rule. Delilah soon tricked him into telling her his great secret. "When he's asleep tonight I will cut off his hair," she whispered to the soldiers. "Then you can safely come into my house and capture him."

Because he had disobeyed God, Samson's great strength was gone, so his enemies cut out his eyes and shut him up in prison.

The Philistines were so pleased they gave a huge party on the flat roof of the house of their god Dagon. Their five kings invited thousands of guests to come and laugh at poor, blind Samson. How they jeered when they looked down and saw him stumbling along, led by a little boy. But they did not realize his hair was growing again—God had forgiven Samson.

"Give me back my strength just one more time," he prayed as he put his arms around the two great pillars which supported the roof.

Suddenly he felt a great surge of power and he pulled until those pillars snapped. Down came the roof and buried him with all the Philistines.

Without their kings and best fighters, the Philistines left the Jews alone for many years. God had needed someone who was brave enough to save his people by dying for them.

THE FOREIGNER

IT WAS HARD living in a strange land far from home. Naomi and her husband had left their farm in God's land because they thought life might be easier for their two sons in a country called Moab. But Naomi never felt happy away from God's people, and she was very miserable when her sons married two girls who did not know God.

Then a dreadful thing happened. Naomi's husband and two sons all died. "Now I'm alone in a foreign land," she sobbed. "I may as well go back home to Bethlehem."

The girl who had married her oldest son kissed her "goodbye" as she left Moab, but the other daughter-in-law, Ruth, put her arms around Naomi's neck and said, "I'll come with you, so you won't be lonely."

"You couldn't do that," replied Naomi nervously. "In my village, they think people from Moab are enemies; they might not be very kind to you."

"But I still can't leave you," said Ruth. "I will turn to your God and love him like you do."

"No one in Bethlehem will help us," warned Naomi.

"We'll have each other," smiled Ruth, and picked up their luggage.

It was harvest time when they arrived, but the two dusty travelers had no money left to buy food. "If we only had some corn we could make some bread," said Ruth. "Tomorrow I'll go into the fields and see if I can pick up any grain the farmers leave."

"Oh no!" replied Naomi, horrified. "The men would hurt you, because you come from Moab and have no husband to care for you."

"But we shall starve if I do nothing," replied Ruth.

All next day Naomi sat in their tumbledown hut praying. She knew how hard it would be for Ruth to work for hours under the burning sun with no food or water to drink and no friends to smile at her. But she did not realize that no one is a foreigner to God. He cares for anyone who turns to him. So he looked after Ruth in a very wonderful way.

She just "happened" to begin looking for corn in the fields of a rich man called Boaz.

He could not stop gazing at her, because she was so beautiful. "That's the foreigner who's been so kind to old Naomi," he thought. "Be kind to that girl," he ordered his workers. "Let her drink from our water jars and leave extra grain lying about for her to find."

Then he called to Ruth and shared his picnic lunch with her. But she was so pretty he could hardly eat anything himself.

"He was the kindest man I ever met," sighed Ruth dreamily when she arrived home with a huge bundle of food.

"God must have led you to his fields," smiled Naomi.

It was not long before Boaz married Ruth, and they took Naomi to live with them in his comfortable house on the hill. For the rest of her life the old lady was happy, helping to care for Ruth's baby son. That little Bethlehem family was to become very special in God's plan.

THE VOICE IN THE NIGHT

HANNAH WAS SO sad, she couldn't eat. "I'll go to God's tent," she thought, "perhaps he can do something to help me." Yet when she got there, she couldn't stop crying.

"What are you doing?" demanded the angry voice of Eli the priest.

"I'm asking God for a baby," sobbed poor Hannah. "If he gives me one, I promise I will bring him back to work for God here when he is old enough."

A few years later the old priest saw her again; this time a little boy was with her.

"Here is Samuel," she said, "the boy God gave to me. Now I am giving him back to God."

Little Samuel loved looking after God's tent, polishing the lamps and sweeping the floors. He loved old Eli too; he was a kind, old man but his two sons were horrid. They did not love God and even stole the presents people brought him.

"I can't let those two go on like this," thought God sadly. "They aren't teaching my people to know me."

One dark night Samuel heard a voice calling him. At first he thought it was Eli and he ran to see what he wanted.

"Go back to bed," Eli told him, "but listen carefully. God is speaking to you." Samuel did not really know God, so he went rather nervously back to his mat in the corner of the great shadowy tent.

In the stillness the voice came again. It really WAS God, and he gave Samuel a terrible message for Eli's nasty sons.

One day a great army of Philistines came marching into the land. The Jews were so frightened, they said: "We'll take the ark from God's tent into battle with us. It might be helpful."

God was furious. He wanted them to trust him, not a golden box! But Eli's sons didn't care, and they ran off carrying the ark.

The message that God had given to Samuel came true. Eli's sons were killed in the fight which followed, and the Philistines stole the ark!

"Dagon is stronger than God," jeered the Philistines as they took the Ark to their temple and placed it in front of the model of Dagon. But that night a dreadful thing happened. The huge statue fell flat on its face before the ark and broke into pieces. The Philistines were so terrified of the ark, they quickly gave it back!

When Samuel grew up, God made him the priest.

"Come and ask God to save us from these Philistines," Samuel told all the people, and thousands of them followed him to a high hill.

But as they prayed, the Philistines were watching them. "Here's our chance," they sneered. "Let's attack them while they're not watching."

When the Jews realized the Philistines were creeping up on them, they were terrified. "Keep on praying!" ordered Samuel. "God will help us."

Suddenly God sent a terrible thunderstorm crashing through the valley. The Philistines were so frightened they ran home, leaving the Jews in peace with Samuel as their leader.

59

THE BOY WHO KILLED A LION

IT WAS VERY DARK up there on the hills above Bethlehem. David the shepherd boy was softly playing his harp and singing to God as he sat guarding his father's sheep. Far away in the valley the lights of his home were twinkling. His great-grandfather, Boaz, had built that house for Ruth, but here on the hills David was quite alone.

Suddenly a twig snapped in the bushes and two, fierce, yellow eyes blinked at him from the shadows. The next minute a huge lion had pounced on one of his favorite lambs.

David jumped up angrily. There was no time to reach for his sling; he simply sprang at the lion, and soon the ferocious creature lay dead. "My brothers will never believe this," smiled David and he comforted his lamb. He had seven big brothers who never thought he was any good at anything.

Next day, Samuel the priest came to the village of Bethlehem. But WHY he had come was a dark secret.

Samuel was an old man now. He had led the people well all his life, but they kept on asking for a proper king. "God is your King," Samuel would tell them.

Still they went on nagging, and finally God had given them Saul.

At first he seemed like a perfect king, but he soon became so proud of himself he didn't bother to keep God's rules.

"Saul keeps on disobeying me," God told Samuel sadly. "He can't be part of my plan.

I will have to give his throne to a man who will teach my people to love me."

That is why Samuel was coming secretly to Bethlehem. God had told him to go and tell a farmer's son there that he would be king one day.

"If Saul finds out, he'll kill me," thought Samuel. "I don't know the name of the man God has chosen, only that his father's called Jesse. But God will need a very powerful man to take Saul's throne."

Samuel was dazzled when he met Jesse's seven, big, tall sons. They looked so brave and strong.

"But none of them will do," said God quietly. "They look fine on the outside, yet I can see they don't love me in their hearts."

Samuel frowned. "Do you happen to have any other sons?" he asked Jesse.

"Oh well," laughed the farmer, "there's little David, the youngest; he's out with the sheep, but he's only a boy."

"Fetch him," ordered Samuel.

As soon as David came running down the hill, God said to Samuel, "This is the one!"

David's big brothers were furious when Samuel told them the secret. "Little David, a king!" they gasped, and when Samuel had gone away they soon sent David back to the sheep again.

But they did not have time to be jealous for long. The Philistines were back causing more trouble. "They say Goliath the giant is with them," they told Jesse. "We must go at once and fight for King Saul."

"Can't I come too?" pleaded David.

"You're far too young," sneered his brothers. "Only men fight giants."

But that is just where they were wrong.

THE TERRIBLE GIANT

DAVID'S HEART pounded with excitement as he hurried along the track. "I might even see a real battle!" he thought.

His brothers had been away so long that their father was very worried. "Take them some food, David," he had said, "and see how they are."

As soon as David arrived at the army camp he knew something was very wrong. Soldiers stood about in anxious huddles, their faces white with fear.

"Whatever is wrong?" demanded David when he found his brothers.

"Look!" they muttered, and with shaking fingers they pointed across the valley. There on top of the hill he stood—the giant Goliath himself, the biggest man in all the world. His great voice boomed and echoed among the rocks and his metal armor flashed in the sunshine.

"Run and hide!" growled David's brothers. "It's been the same every day for weeks. He stands there daring one of us to go and fight him."

"Your God's no good!" roared the giant scornfully.

"Why *doesn't* someone fight him?" demanded David. "He can't talk about God like that!"

"You stupid little boy!" snapped David's oldest brother. "Can't you see he's enormous?"

"Yes, but God's on our side!" protested David. "I'll go myself if no one else will."

Goliath positively shook with laughter when he saw a boy hurrying towards him carrying a sling. All the Jewish soldiers looked on in horror, and King Saul held his breath.

"You come against me with a sword and a spear," called David, "but I come with the power of God! I'll show the whole world how great he is!"

"I'll give your body to the birds for their dinner," yelled Goliath and charged with his massive spear at David.

David pulled a pebble from his bag and carefully took aim. He knew he could not afford to miss with that angry giant crashing towards him!

Goliath's great mouth was open wide as he roared with mocking laughter, but through the air came a little stone and it hit him between the eyes. Suddenly the laughter stopped. The gigantic spear was nearly touching David when Goliath

staggered and crashed to the ground flat on his face. All the watching Philistines gasped with horror and David's brothers stood gazing in surprise. Hastily David darted forward, picked up the giant's sword and hacked off his ugly head.

With screams of terror the Philistines began to run for their lives, with the Jewish soldiers after them.

"You can't be a shepherd any more," King Saul said to David. "Come back to my palace with me and you shall marry my daughter."

All the way home girls came dancing out of every village they passed, clapping, cheering and throwing flowers at David the giant-killer.

"They like him more than they like me now!" thought King Saul, and because the king began to feel jealous, David was in danger.

THE MAN THE KING COULD NOT KILL

THE KING WAS in a terrible temper and everyone in the palace was scared. "Quick! Play your harp and quiet him down," they whispered to David.

Life was very different for the shepherd boy now. The king's son Jonathan was his best friend and all the people in the land loved David. That was really what made Saul so jealous.

Suddenly a spear the king had been holding whizzed through the air towards David's head. He dropped the harp and just in time ducked out of the way, while the spear crashed into the wall behind him.

"I'll kill you somehow!" fumed the king, and sent David off to fight a dangerous pack of Philistines. But David killed them all and came back smiling.

"Go to David's house," Saul snarled at some of his men, "and jump on him when he comes out in the morning." Fortunately David's wife, the princess, saw them standing in the shadows and smuggled him away in time.

"You're not being fair to David," protested Prince Jonathan, but his father threw a spear at him too and forced David's wife to marry another man.

Wherever David went, Saul chased after him, and whoever helped him was in terrible trouble. In the end, there was nowhere left for David to go but the desert, and there he lived in a cave among the rocks. Many people who were tired of Saul's cruelty came to keep him company.

"I'll kill them all!" roared Saul and set off with an army of three thousand men.

One day, after they had been clanking around in their armor for weeks, Saul went into a cave to rest. Little did he know that it was the very cave where David and his men were hiding.

"Here's your chance," whispered David's friends. "Kill him and be king yourself, just as God promised."

Silently David slipped through the dark cave and, with his sharp sword, cut off the corner of Saul's coat. Then he melted into the shadows once again. "It would be breaking God's rules to hurt him," he explained to his astonished men.

Saul was calmly walking away up the valley with his soldiers when he was amazed to hear David's voice shouting at him from the cliffs. "Your Majesty! What happened to your coat?" Saul was so surprised he was speechless. "I could have killed you just now," went on David, "but I didn't. Now will you believe I don't want to harm you? I promise I will always be good to you and your family."

Saul went home to his palace feeling rather silly, but he was soon back hunting among the rocks for his enemy again.

In the end poor David had to escape to the land of the Philistines, and it was while he was there he heard the terrible news. Saul and Prince Jonathan had been killed in a battle with thousands of other Jews.

It was time for him to march back home and become the kind of king God had planned for his people.

THE LAME PRINCE

QUICK! RUN! The battle is lost, the Philistines are coming!" That was the cry that rang through Saul's palace the dreadful day that he and the prince were killed.

Jonathan's little boy, Mephibosheth, was playing happily with his toys when his nurse scooped him up in terror. "I'll take you to my home in the hills," she gasped. "The Philistines mustn't kill you too."

Unfortunately she ran so fast she tripped, and the prince fell heavily to the ground. His legs were badly crushed but she picked him up again and ran on blindly.

As the years went by Mephibosheth grew up, hidden in the lonely hut, but his legs were twisted and useless and he had to hop about on crutches.

Soon the new King David had driven all the Philistines from the land, but poor Mephibosheth was still afraid.

"If David ever finds you," his nurse would say, "he will certainly kill you, because of all the cruel things your grandfather Saul did to him."

"He must never find me!" gasped the little prince. But one dreadful day David's servants came and took him to the palace.

Mephibosheth was far too frightened to look up at the great king on his throne, but

when David spoke his voice sounded very kind. "Years ago I promised Jonathan that I would always be good to his family," he said. "So if you like, you can live here with me in the palace forever." David was always doing kind things like that, and everyone loved him.

David built a grand, new city, called Jerusalem, on a high hill. Because David enjoyed worshiping God more than anything else, he longed to have God's great tent pitched there in his city. But one thing worried him terribly. The golden ark was missing. Dreadful things happened to the Philistines when they had stolen it. So when they gave it back, no one dared to touch it or go near it, and it had been left on a farm.

"I'll go myself and fetch it!" said King David, but he was forgetting that God had said *NO ONE* except the priests should ever carry that precious box. It was far too holy.

David's soldiers loaded it carelessly onto a cart, but when one of the oxen stumbled it nearly fell off the back and all the soldiers roared with laughter.

"Steady there," grinned Uzzah and put out his hand to touch the ark. No one, not even a priest, should ever have done that, and instantly he fell dead. David and all his men were terrified and went home leaving the ark behind.

"We have to learn to do EXACTLY as God says," whispered David. "We were forgetting how great he really is."

Three months later a marvelous procession entered Jerusalem. Bands played, crowds cheered and people danced and sang. This time they did everything just right, and it was the priests who carried the ark.

David was the greatest king the Jews ever had, and while he lived they were peaceful and happy because they all tried hard to keep God's rules.

WHEN DAVID BROKE THE RULES

NO ONE THOUGHT King David could ever do anything bad. But one day he did. It all started just because he was feeling lazy. David SHOULD have gone off to war with his soldiers, but he stayed at home instead.

One warm evening as he stood looking over the city from his palace roof, he saw something which made him gaze in wonder. A beautiful woman was bathing in her swimming pool. Her name was Bathsheba, and her husband was one of the king's soldiers.

David had lots of wives, but he still fell in love with her, and soon she found she was to have his baby.

"Her husband mustn't find out," thought David in a panic. So he sent a secret message to his general, telling him to put Bathsheba's husband, Uriah, right at the front of the battle, just where the Philistines would be sure to kill him. When they heard that Uriah had died fighting bravely, David and Bathsheba were married.

But naturally God was very sad, and when the baby was born he sent his prophet Nathan to the palace. "I have a message from God for you," he said to the king, and David settled down to listen carefully.

"There were once two men," began Nathan. "One was very rich and had thousands of sheep. The other was miserably poor; all his family had was one pet lamb that they loved dearly. One day the rich man wanted a treat for a visitor's dinner, but instead of eating one of his own animals, he killed the poor man's pet lamb

and left him and all his children crying bitterly. Now, Your Majesty, was that a fair thing to do?"

"No," thundered the king, "that rich man should die!"

"*YOU* are that man!" answered the prophet. "You have many wives; Uriah only had one. Yet you stole her and then had him killed. You broke two of God's rules and he is very angry."

Just then David's servants rushed in to tell him Bathsheba's baby was very ill. For a whole week David was so worried he ate nothing, but lay face downwards on the floor of his bedroom.

"However shall we tell him?" whispered David's servants when at last the baby died. "He'll never get over this."

The king heard them muttering and he guessed what had happened. "I'll go and tell God how I feel," he thought and went off to God's tent.

Because David was sorry for the bad things he had done, God forgave him, and David walked home feeling happy once again. "My baby is safe in heaven," he said. "One day I shall see him again."

Soon God let David and Bathsheba have another baby, and from the moment he was born, God loved Solomon in a very special way.

"He shall be king one day, when I am gone," smiled David, "and God will make him great."

God also told David about his secret plan: "One day, many years from now, a King will be born in your family who will rule the world for ever."

THE WISEST MAN IN THE WORLD

IT'S JUST NOT right, Solomon!" said King David to his son. "I live in a beautiful palace, and God only has a tent. I've always wanted to build him the most wonderful house in the world, but he said he would rather *you* built it for him one day."

"Me!" protested the prince nervously. "I wouldn't even know how to start."

"I am old now," replied David, "but I will spend the rest of my life collecting gold, silver, cedar wood and marble so, when I am gone, everything will be ready."

It was a great day when Solomon was crowned king. But that night he went to bed feeling very worried. "I'm only a young man," he thought, "and my father has left me so many people to rule I can't even count them. And how can I possibly build this wonderful temple?"

When at last he fell asleep, God spoke to him in a dream. "Solomon," said God, "I want to give you whatever you want."

Solomon *was* surprised. Should he ask to be amazingly rich, or for a long, healthy life without any enemies?

Then suddenly he knew just what he wanted most of all. "Please, God," he said simply, "could you make me very wise so I can lead your people well."

God was so pleased he had asked for wisdom that he gave Solomon all the other things as well! Soon he was the richest king in the world and everyone was talking about the golden temple that he built for God.

He was also very kind and always had time to help his people. One day two very angry women came to his palace to ask him to settle their argument. They were each carrying a baby, but one of the babies was dead.

"We both sleep in the same room," began the first woman. "In the night *her* baby died, so she stole mine while I slept and put her dead one in it's place."

"That's not true!" cried the other woman. "It was *her* baby who died."

One of them was telling lies, but which one was it?

"Guard!" called Solomon. "Bring your sword and cut the living baby in two. Give them half each!"

"Yes, that's fair," said the first woman quickly, but the other one could not bear the baby to be killed. "Let her have him," she screamed, "anything is better than having him hurt."

"You must be the real mother," smiled Solomon. "Put away your sword, guard, and give the baby to the woman who really loves him."

"Solomon's God must be powerful to make him such a great king," said people all over the world, and many of them traveled thousands of miles to find out all about God and worship in Solomon's temple. God's great plan seemed to be working wonderfully, but his old enemy Satan was still busy.

THE WICKED QUEEN

YOUR GOD'S no good," sneered the new Queen Jezebel as she swept into the palace followed by all her servants. "Baal is the god of our country; you will all worship him now."

"Yes, dear," muttered her husband, King Ahab, "I'll build a temple for his statue at once." It was his wedding day, but already he was scared of his new wife!

Of course Ahab should never have married a princess from a foreign land. God said the Jews could only marry people who followed him. But since Solomon had died, God's rules were being forgotten.

"Baal will send your farmers all the sun and rain they need," said Jezebel, "so long as you let me kill anyone who will not bow down to his statue."

"All right, dear," nodded Ahab, and tried not to notice her servants marching around his land cutting off people's heads. But Satan was telling Jezebel what to do, and he was delighted when she made people too frightened to love God.

Ahab was lying comfortably in his palace one afternoon when he had a nasty shock. A strange looking man pushed his way into the room and stood glaring down at him.

"Who are you?" gasped the king. The palace servants were always dressed beautifully, but this man wore an old, animal skin cloak and looked as if he never brushed his hair.

"I am God's prophet, Elijah," boomed the man. "He has sent me to tell you he is tired of being forgotten, so it will not rain again until he says it may."

"Baal controls the weather!" shouted Ahab. "Guards!" But Elijah was off to the hills long before they could catch him.

No rain fell that year, so no crops would grow. The next summer all the streams and lakes began to dry up, and the people were thirsty as well as hungry. The year after that thousands of them died.

"Why doesn't Baal do something?" muttered Ahab.

"Find that Elijah person," ordered Jezebel. "He's caused all this."

"Yes, dear," muttered Ahab, and sent his soldiers off to search the whole world for Elijah.

But God had hidden him completely, and it was three years before he sent him back to Ahab.

"I've just seen Elijah!" gasped one of the king's servants as he hurried to the palace. "He's coming here now!"

"Here?" spluttered the king. "Jezebel will kill him if she finds out."

"Just look what you've done to my people!" he bellowed when Elijah arrived. "They're dying of hunger."

"YOU'RE the one who caused their trouble," said Elijah sternly, "by leading them away from God. Tell them all to go to that mountain over there and I will prove to them once and for all that Baal is pretend and God is real."

"Jezebel won't like that," said Ahab nervously.

"If you want rain, you will do just as I say," replied Elijah, and strode out of the palace.

FIRE FROM THE SKY

SOMETHING VERY strange was happening on top of the mountain that day. Baal's prophets were dancing around and around shouting and cutting themselves with knives.

Ever since dawn, thousands of hungry people had been dragging themselves up there to watch what was going to happen. Even King Ahab was looking on from his chariot.

"Today you will know who is real, God or Baal," Elijah had told everyone. "Whoever can send down fire from the sky is the god you should follow."

"Oh Baal, hear us!" howled Jezebel's prophets, as hour after hour they danced in circles under the hot sun.

"Shout a bit louder," laughed Elijah. "Perhaps Baal's thinking, or maybe he's asleep!"

"Send down fire," screamed his prophets until their throats hurt and they had no breath left.

King Ahab was looking very embarrassed by the end of the day, and when the tired prophets had flopped to the ground, Elijah said to everyone, "Baal is only a wooden statue. Of course he can't send fire, but God can." Then he took a bull as a present for God and laid it ready on a pile of wood. "Go and fetch buckets of water," he told the people, "and pour it over the wood."

Ahab smiled when he saw what they were doing. "No fire will ever be able to burn such wet wood," he sneered. But Elijah did not have to dance and shout to make God hear him. He simply looked up and said, "Lord, prove now how powerful you are."

As the people held their breath, hardly daring to look, a great fireball exploded in the sky. It burnt up the sacrifice and all the dripping wet wood. It split the stones and scorched the earth and the people flung themselves down on their faces. "The Lord alone is God!" they shouted.

Jezebel's prophets were huddled in a frightened heap. "Take them down the mountain and kill them all!" ordered Elijah, and they did so at once.

King Ahab was eating his picnic tea when Elijah went back alone up the mountain to pray for rain.

Suddenly, over the sea he saw a tiny cloud and heard the distant rumble of thunder. "Here comes the rain!" he shouted. "Hurry home, King Ahab, before you get wet."

The thunder was crashing overhead and the wind was howling as Elijah ran along in front of Ahab's chariot. People lined the road all the way, cheering as the rain fell on the dry ground. They did not mind getting wet at all; they hadn't had a wash for three years! "The Lord, he is God," they kept on shouting as they splashed in the puddles.

But back in the palace Queen Jezebel was waiting, and she was livid. "These people shall not turn back to their God!" she hissed. "By this time tomorrow I will have killed Elijah."

STORM ON THE MOUNTAIN

ELIJAH HUDDLED in the darkness of the cave; he was so miserable he wanted to die. Just when he thought he had turned the people back to God, everything had gone wrong, and now Jezebel was hunting everywhere for him again.

For weeks he had forced himself to go on walking through the lonely desert, and now he was hiding on Sinai, God's holy mountain. Perhaps here he would find out why Jezebel and her friend Satan always seemed to win. But it was a lonely, frightening place and he shivered in the damp cave.

"What are you doing here, Elijah?" God's voice made him jump.

A terrible wind hurled itself at the mountain, and an earthquake made the boulders rumble and shake. Fire spurted from cracks in the rocks and the whole of Sinai seemed to be trembling. Elijah covered his face with his cloak and stood at the mouth of the cave.

"Why have you come here"? asked God again.

When he spoke his voice was just a soft, gentle whisper, and suddenly the frightened prophet felt safe and comforted. God was more powerful than hurricanes and earthquakes, so he could easily deal with Jezebel.

"Lord, all your people have broken the pact you made with them here on this mountain long ago," replied Elijah. "No one keeps your rules now, and I'm the only prophet they haven't killed yet."

"Don't worry," replied God kindly. "My plans have not gone wrong. I have already chosen a man called Jehu to be King instead of Ahab's wicked family."

"But I'm the only person left who still loves you," said poor Elijah.

"No," replied God, "I have many secret friends who never bow to Baal. I am going to turn my people back to me again, but you will need someone to help you to teach them how to love me. I have chosen a young man called Elisha. Go now and show him how to be my prophet."

A farmer was busy plowing his fields, one day, when a strange looking man walked straight up to him. Without saying a word, the man took off his cloak and threw it over the farmer's shoulders.

Elisha stopped still and the oxen pulled the plow on without him. "You must be the great prophet Elijah," he gasped. "Giving me your cloak like that means you want me to follow you."

"You will have to leave your farm and your parents if you do," said the old prophet. "When we walk around the land telling people about God, you will never have a proper home, and Queen Jezebel may even kill you."

"I'll go and kiss my parents goodbye at once," smiled Elisha. "I've always wanted to be God's prophet."

They must have looked an odd pair as they tramped away together. Elijah had long, untidy hair and a sad face, while Elisha was quite bald and always smiling. Yet they became very good friends, because God uses all kinds of different people in his plans.

THE SULKY KING

"IT'S NOT FAIR!" sulked Ahab, and he turned over in bed to face the wall. "Whatever is the matter?" demanded Jezebel, bursting into his bedroom. "You haven't eaten any dinner."

"It's that farmer Naboth, next door," whined the king. "His land would make a lovely garden for me, but he won't sell it."

"Are you the king or not?" snapped Jezebel. "Get up at once. I'll get your garden for you."

"Yes, dear," muttered Ahab.

"If Naboth and all his sons were dead," whispered Jezebel wickedly, "his farm would belong to the king...so..." and she hurried off to write some letters.

When she had finished, she carefully signed her husband's name at the bottom of each one and gave them to her servants. "Take these letters to all the most important men in the city," she told them. "They are from the king himself."

In those letters she told all kinds of lies about poor Naboth, who happened to be one of God's secret friends. "Tell everyone how bad this farmer is," she ordered. "Make them throw stones at him and his family until they're dead."

A few days later a messenger brought her a reply, which made her smile until the paint on her face began to crack. "Go and plan your garden, Ahab," she called. "The wild dogs are licking up Naboth's blood outside the city gates."

"Yes, dear," replied Ahab, but somehow he felt uncomfortable as he walked through the farm gate. Someone was watching him through the leaves of the grapevine, and suddenly he saw the prophet Elijah. "He's always there when I don't want him," growled the king.

"God sent me to tell you he has seen all the bad things you and Jezebel have done," said Elijah. "He is going to sweep away you and your sons, and just as the dogs licked the blood of Naboth, so they will also lick your blood."

Not long after that, new enemies called the Syrians attacked the land. Ahab was terrified. "I can't ride off to war in my crown and best purple robes," he protested. "Those Syrians are bound to kill me when they know I'm the king." So he borrowed an old chariot and some ordinary armor from one of his soldiers and went off to battle in disguise.

The Syrians soon became tired of looking for Ahab, so they began to shoot arrows just anywhere. One of them flew through the air and found a chink in Ahab's armor. By the end of the day he was dead, and the wild dogs were licking his blood just as God said that they would.

"Never mind," said Jezebel, "my son will do as I tell him, just as his father always did."

But God had not finished with Jezebel yet.

A CHARIOT FROM THE SKY

"YOU DON'T HAVE to come any further," said Elijah to his friend as they walked along the road together. "You know God is taking me home to heaven soon, and you'll only be sad."

"I'm not leaving you," replied poor Elisha as the tears ran down his round face.

On and on they walked, visiting all the colleges that Elijah had built to teach men how to be prophets.

"How shall we all manage without him?" thought Elisha miserably.

At last they reached the banks of the great Jordan River. "You'll never cross the water at this time of year," said some of the young prophets from the Jericho college.

Silently Elijah took off his old cloak and used it to hit the fast flowing water.

Instantly the current stopped and he and Elisha walked over the dry riverbed.

"Something amazing is about to happen," said the young prophets as they stood watching on the river bank.

Elijah knew how sad his poor friend was feeling. "What can I give you, now that I am going to God?" he said kindly.

"Please leave me your power," replied Elisha miserably, "so that I can teach people about God too."

Just then, out of the sky plunged horses of fire. They swept between the two men, pulling a flaming chariot behind them. Elijah sprang in, and a mighty whirlwind carried him safely to heaven. But as he waved goodbye, his cloak flew from his shoulders and swirled down through the sky. Slowly Elisha picked it up and put it on.

80

Did this really mean that God had chosen him to be a great prophet like Elijah? He still was not sure until he reached the banks of the river once again. Could he stop the water, as Elijah had done? The fifty young men were still standing there gazing at him in wonder as he hit the river with his master's cloak.

"The power of Elijah is upon him," they gasped as they watched him walk over the dry river bed. "Come into Jericho and rest," they murmured as they bowed to their new leader.

But there was no rest for anyone in Jericho; it was in chaos. A terrible illness was sweeping the city. People shuffled about the streets crying loudly, and in every home someone was ill or dying.

"We think the water in our well has gone bad," the city leaders told Elisha. "Whatever can we do about it?"

Standing by the well, Elisha asked God for help. Then he threw some salt down into the water below. "God says he has made the water safe now," he smiled.

"Salt in drinking water!" scoffed the followers of Baal. But after that no one else was sick or died when they drank from the well of Jericho.

Queen Jezebel was delighted when she heard in her palace that Elijah had gone for ever. But she had not heard about Elisha then!

THE SEVEN SNEEZES

WHAT'S THE POINT of being rich, if you can't have what you want most of all?" thought a very grand lady as she stood at the window of her fine house. She had always longed for a baby, but now it was impossible. Her husband was too old.

"Oh look!" she said suddenly. "There's that man again. He often comes to our village, telling people about God."

It was Elisha who was trudging past on the road, and he looked dusty and tired.

"Husband," said the rich lady, "may I ask him to supper?" She loved God, so she often did kind things.

"Something amazing happened last week," Elisha told them as they were eating. "I met a poor widow who was crying bitterly. A cruel man was going to take away her two little boys and make them his slaves, because she couldn't pay back the money he had lent her."

"Why not?" asked the rich lady.

"Because all she had left in the world was a little jar of oil," Elisha answered. "So I told her to borrow lots of bowls and basins, and God made her tiny drop of oil fill them all. We sold it at market for so much money that when that man came to grab her boys, she paid him everything she owed. He was furious!" added Elisha with a huge smile. "Now they have enough money to live on until the boys grow up."

Soon Elisha was visiting the fine house so often, they built him his own little bedroom. He was so grateful he asked what he could do for them in return.

"We have everything we need," replied the lady, who was much too shy to tell anyone how sad she really felt. But Elisha's servant, Gehazi, guessed her secret and whispered something in his master's ear.

"Next year you will hold a baby son in your arms," beamed Elisha.

"Don't tease me!" gasped the lady, but Elisha was quite right.

As the little boy grew up he was always looking out of the window, hoping Elisha would come along the road. He loved to hear the story of the chariot in the sky. But one dreadful day he became very ill. "My head hurts," he moaned, and, while he was sitting on his mother's lap, he died.

"I must find Elisha!" she cried as she laid the boy on the prophet's bed, and, jumping on her fastest donkey, she rode off like a whirlwind.

Elisha was praying on top of a mountain, and he saw her coming from miles away in a cloud of dust. "Something is wrong!" he said to Gehazi.

A few hours later Elisha was standing alone in his tiny bedroom, praying to God as he gazed down at the stiff, cold, little body.

Outside the door Gehazi and the lady waited anxiously, and they could hardly believe their ears when they heard the little boy sneeze seven times. Then the door burst open and there was Elisha, holding him by the hand.

The rich lady scooped her son into her arms, too happy to say anything, and Elisha's smile grew bigger than ever.

THE PROUD GENERAL

"THE SYRIANS are attacking again," snapped Queen Jezebel. "They keep stealing our children to be their slaves. Do something!"

"Yes, Mother," replied her son the king, "but we're all too frightened of Naaman, their army general."

The queen snorted and went off to paint her face.

Far away in the land of Syria, Naaman, the fierce soldier, was having a bath. "Look!" he bellowed in horror. His wife and all the servants rushed in, and there on his chest was a tiny white patch.

"LEPROSY!" they screamed as they realized he would soon become very ill, and then die.

"Whatever shall we do?" cried Naaman's wife. But a small hand was pulling her dress. There stood the little Jewish slave girl who had worked for her ever since she had been stolen from her own home. "In my land," whispered the child, "there's a prophet of God who makes sick people well."

"I'll go there at once!" said Naaman, and jumped out of the bath.

Some time later, when a huge train of chariots and horses pulled up outside Jezebel's palace, her son was really worried. "Naaman says he's come to be cured!" he stormed. "No one can heal leprosy, so he'll probably kill us all!" He was so upset he jumped off his throne and ripped his robes to pieces!

Just then a message arrived from Elisha. "Send this man to me. I'll show you both what God can do."

Naaman felt far too important to be sent off to some back street. His horses and neighbors stare. Naaman became angry when Elisha did not even bother to come out himself; he simply sent Gehazi to the door with another message. The bulging chests of gold and silver Naaman had brought to pay for his cure made Gehazi's mouth turn dry. "My master says if you will bathe seven times in the Jordan River you will be well," he said as he gazed at the money.

"Bathe in that muddy, smelly water!" spluttered Naaman. "Never!" And he rode off in such a rage it took his servant a long time to calm him enough to try the prophet's cure.

As Naaman slithered out of the river for the seventh time he realized he was perfectly well. "Now I know there's a God!" he exclaimed as he burst into Elisha's house. "Slaves! Bring in the reward!"

But to Gehazi's horror he heard his master say, "God has made you well, so I will take nothing."

"Never again," murmured the general, "will I ever bow down to statues. Only your God is real." And he rode home well and happy, all because a little slave girl was part of God's plan.

But Gehazi just could not bear to see all that money rumbling away. "I don't care about God anymore," he thought. "I just want to be rich." So he ran after Naaman. "My master's changed his mind," he lied, and was soon hiding the heavy bags of treasure.

But Elisha knew just what he had done, and before Gehazi could enjoy his money his body was covered all over with Naaman's leprosy.

THE BLIND SOLDIERS

ONE OF YOU is a traitor!" roared the King of Syria as he brought his fist thundering down on the table. All his army captains and advisers shook with fear as they looked helplessly at one another. "No one can hear what we're saying in this room," went on the king, "yet every time we make a surprise attack on the Jews they seem to know just when we're coming. One of you must be telling them all our secrets."

"No, Your Majesty," faltered one man at last. "We're not spies, but Elisha the prophet of God seems to know everything. He tells his king exactly what we are planning!"

"We can't win a war with a man like that against us!" bellowed the king of Syria. "Send an army to bring him here."

Naaman must have refused to fight against God's people anymore, so a new general marched off boldly, followed by a troop of his bravest soldiers.

"Elisha is in Dothan," they were told, and just as darkness fell they reached the little town.

"Spread out around the walls," ordered the general, "and then camp for the night."

Early next morning Elisha's new servant got up and climbed the wall. "Master!" he gasped. "Look! Thousands of soldiers! Whatever shall we do?"

"It's all right," yawned the prophet sleepily as he looked through a slit in the wall. "We have more on our side than they have."

"But we haven't any soldiers at all!" protested the boy.

"Lord, open his eyes," prayed Elisha, and the boy gasped in amazement when he suddenly saw millions of angels surrounding the town.

"They're always there looking after us," smiled the prophet, "but usually we can't see them."

As Elisha opened the city gates and walked calmly out, the Syrian general shouted, "Seize him!" But Elisha was praying again, and instantly every one of those soldiers became blind. They dropped their swords and shields and began groping about in the darkness.

"You haven't come to the right town," called Elisha to the blind general. "Come with me; I'll lead you to the man you want."

Queen Jezebel and her son the king stood on the walls of Samaria, gazing in amazement. There, striding towards them, was Elisha, and groping their way along behind him came the Syrian soldiers. They were all holding hands to stop themselves from falling into ditches or getting lost. Right into the king's city they came, and the gates slammed shut behind them.

"Let them see again now, Lord," prayed Elisha. How surprised they looked when they realized where they were.

"Shall we kill them all?" giggled the King.

"Certainly not!" snorted Elisha. "That wouldn't be fair. Give them some food and then send them home."

"They actually fed you?" boomed the king of Syria when he heard the story. "I should have listened to Naaman. Their God is too powerful for us." For a long time after that he did not dare to attack the Jews again.

NOTHING LEFT TO EAT

ELISHA IS A troublemaker!" snarled Queen Jezebel. Yet it was because she would not let the people turn back to God that he allowed the Syrians to attack them once again.

Up to Samaria they marched and put up their tents all around the city.

"They'll never get in here," sniffed the queen scornfully. "Our walls are far too thick."

"Yes, but we're trapped," protested the king. "If we can't get out to fetch any food we'll starve."

He was right. Soon there was so little food in the city, people were dying. Still the queen would not let them ask God for help. "It's all Elisha's fault," she raged. "Send soldiers to kill him."

"Yes, Mother," muttered the king. But when the soldiers had gone he thought, "If Mother's wrong, God will be angry with me." Picking up his robes he dashed through the streets after them, with his chief adviser puffing along behind him. He was just in time to find them hammering at the door of Elisha's house.

"God says, by this time tomorrow there will be more food in the city than we can possibly eat!" boomed Elisha when he opened the door.

The chief adviser, who was Jezebel's friend, snorted rudely, and Elisha turned to him. "Because you don't believe what God says, you will not be there to enjoy the food he sends," said the prophet sternly.

Outside the city gate sat four, cold, ragged men. No one wanted them because they had leprosy, and everyone was frightened of catching it too.

"We'll die of hunger if we sit here much longer," they said miserably. "Let's go to the Syrians' tents. They might give us a crust of bread before they kill us." So when it was dark, they set off.

"It's empty!" they whispered as they looked inside the first tent. "But look at all that lovely food."

Soon they were stuffing themselves until they could hardly move. Then they dressed up in grand clothes and grabbed the money and jewels that lay scattered around.

"Something must be wrong," one of them whispered suddenly. "It's too quiet here. Where ARE all the Syrians?"

From tent to tent they crept, but each one was completely empty.

"They've gone," chuckled one of the lepers. "We're rich!"

"But they're starving back in the city," said another. "Aren't we being mean to keep this good news to ourselves?"

"We are," the others agreed, and they began to run towards the gates.

The reason why all the tents were empty was because God had made the Syrians imagine the sound of thousands of soldiers and horses marching towards them. They had been so terrified, they had all run away leaving everything behind.

At first no one believed the lepers' story. "It's a trick," they said. "The Syrians are just hiding in the dark, waiting to pounce on us."

But when they found their footprints running back towards Syria, everyone rushed out of the gates at once.

The king's chief adviser, who had laughed at Elisha, fell over and was trampled to death. As Elisha had said, he would never enjoy the food God promised.

"I still won't care about God!" growled Jezebel, "and neither shall my son."

THE END OF WICKED QUEEN JEZEBEL

JEZEBEL SAT in front of her mirror, painting her face. She was getting very old, but she did not want anyone to know that. There were two kings in God's land now. One was Jezebel's son; he ruled the north. The other king lived in Jerusalem and he ruled the south. Jezebel had married her daughter to him because she wanted to be able to tell both kings what to do. She thought she had been very clever, but her time was running out.

Yet another war was going on with Syria, and the two kings joined together to fight.

When Jezebel's son was scratched by a sword he made such a fuss they both rushed home to Jezebel.

"Fancy having a holiday in the middle of a war," scoffed their soldiers in disgust. "Our General Jehu would make a much better king!" God thought so too, and one day when the general and his officers were planning their next battle, in walked a strange looking young man.

"I have a message from God," he said to Jehu. "He is making YOU king instead of Jezebel's wicked family, so you can destroy the statues of Baal and all who bow to them."

Jehu always did everything in a hurry, so he sprang straight into his chariot and galloped away like the wind.

"Look!" gasped the two kings as they looked out of Jezebel's palace. "See that cloud of dust? No one but Jehu rides as fast as that. He must bring news of the war."

They jumped on to their horses and rode out to meet him. How surprised they must have been when Jehu began to shoot them with his arrows.

Jezebel's son fell off his horse and died in the very field his mother had once stolen from Naboth.

The king from the south turned his frightened horse for home, but he was dead long before he reached Jerusalem.

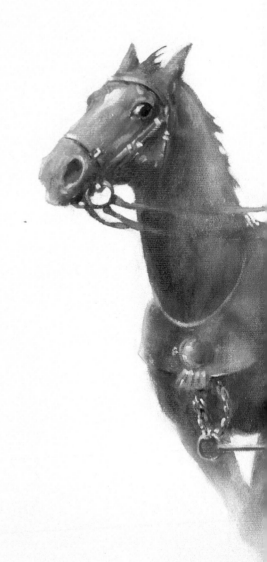

"Jehu shall die!" fumed Jezebel as she watched from her bedroom window. But her servants were so pleased to see a new king riding bravely up to the door of the palace that they threw her down from the window and she died on the stones below. While everyone was having dinner, the wild dogs came and ate her up, just as Elijah said they would.

Jehu sat down on his new throne and thought very hard. "How am I going to know which people follow Baal?" he wondered. "They'll all hide from me now." Then he had a very clever idea.

Soon everyone who bowed to Baal was whispering some wonderful news. "The new King Jehu says he wants to worship Baal with us. He's invited us all to a special service."

From all over the country they came, dressed in their special robes, and they crammed themselves into Baal's temple. Jehu and his soldiers dressed up too, but under their robes they had each hidden a sword. Before the service was over, everyone who followed Baal was dead.

"We'll turn this temple into a public toilet," laughed Jehu as he threw all the ugly statues into the bonfire.

All God's secret friends were allowed to worship him again, but down in the south things were very different. Jezebel's daughter was the queen and she was furious.

THE HIDDEN PRINCE

JEZEBEL'S DAUGHTER, Athaliah, was even more wicked than her mother. She snapped her fingers in glee when she heard that her son had been killed by Jehu. "Now I shall be queen," she hissed.

"But Your Majesty," protested her servants, "it is the law for one of your other sons to be king now."

"Kill them all!" she ordered. "And my grandsons too. No one will rule this land but me."

While soldiers ran through the palace killing all the princes, Jehoiada the priest lay on the stone floor of the temple, crying as he prayed to God. It was dark and lonely in the great building, for most people in Jerusalem were too frightened of the queen to worship God.

Suddenly he heard a rustle in the shadows behind him. Jumping up he saw his wife creeping in, carrying a tiny bundle. "Where can we hide this little prince?" she sobbed. "All his brothers and uncles are dead. I smuggled him out of the palace just in time." Quickly they took the baby to a secret room at the back of the temple.

No one else knew baby Joash was still alive. So for seven years he lived in that little room, hidden from his evil grandmother.

He grew to love the old priest and his wife, who told him all about God. "He has kept you safe, so that one day you will be part of his plan," the old man said.

Life with Athaliah as queen was terrible and, after seven years, Jehoiada the priest knew it was time her cruelty was finished. Secretly he called to the temple all the most important people in the land. From all directions they came, creeping past the palace so that the queen should not see them and wonder what was happening.

There was hardly room to breathe when everyone was squashed inside the temple. "Whatever could the priest have to say?" they wondered. "And why had he handed out all the old swords and spears that once belonged to King David?"

"Would you like to see your true king?" Jehoiada asked in the hushed silence. There was a gasp of amazement when he led little Joash out of his hiding place.

"We thought he was dead," they whispered as they watched the priest place the crown on the small boy's head.

"Here is a copy of God's rules," said Jehoiada, handing Joash a scroll. "If you keep them, you will be a good king."

No one could stay quiet any longer after that. The trumpets blew and people clapped and cheered.

"What's that noise?" demanded Athaliah, and she hurried from her palace to see what was going on. There, at the top of the temple steps, stood her little grandson surrounded by men with drawn swords. "Treason!" she screamed in a dreadful rage, but they dragged her out of the temple and killed her.

Little Joash was led through cheering crowds to the palace and lifted onto the throne.

The people were free to worship God once again in Jerusalem, just as they were up in the north in Samaria. The little king grew up loving the temple where he had been hidden for so long.

INSIDE A FISH

BUT GOD! The Assyrians are dreadful people! Surely you don't love them?" spluttered the prophet Jonah in disgust.

"I do," replied God. "Go to their wicked city Nineveh and tell them if they don't change their ways I will have to destroy them all."

"I'm not doing that!" thought Jonah crossly. "They're our enemies; I WANT them destroyed!"

So instead of crossing the desert to Nineveh, as God had told him, he jumped onto a ship going in quite the opposite direction. He was forgetting that you can't run away from God; he is everywhere.

"I'll soon be safe in Spain," he thought as he fell happily to sleep. But when he woke a dreadful storm had hit the ship. It creaked and groaned as the huge waves crashed over the decks and the wind screamed round the mast.

"We're going to sink!" cried the sailors.

"God must be angry with me," thought Jonah, "because I disobeyed him." "Throw me overboard," he shouted to the captain. "This storm is all my fault."

Down and down sank Jonah, under the raging waves. Salt water choked him and seaweed tangled around his head.

"I'm going to die," he thought. But God had already planned for a great fish to swim along and swallow him just in time.

It's not much fun inside a fish's tummy— very dark and smelly. But as soon as Jonah told God how very sorry he was, the fish swam ashore and was very sick on the beach.

"Now off you go to Nineveh," said God.

"Oh no!" grumbled Jonah, but this time he did not dare to disobey.

"In forty days time God will wipe you all away," he shouted above the noise of Nineveh's busy streets. Crowds gathered around him and soon they began to cry. When the king heard what Jonah was saying, he climbed down from his golden throne and, taking off his fine robes, he covered himself in a dirty old sack.

"No one in the city must eat or drink," he ordered. "Everyone must pray that God will forgive us."

As soon as God heard their prayers and saw how sorry they all were, he changed his mind and decided not to destroy the city after all.

Jonah WAS cross. "I knew this would happen," he grumbled. "God is just too kind. These dreadful people deserved to die."

Angrily he left Nineveh and climbed a high hill nearby, still hoping to see the city

burned to the ground. But of course nothing happened.

The sun beat down on him and gave him a headache. He felt sick, thirsty and crosser than ever. "I wish I was dead," he thought. "This is worse than the fish's tummy."

"Why are you so angry with me?" God's voice made Jonah jump. "I made all those people down in that city, just as I made you."

Jonah sat and thought about that for a long time; then he walked all the way home and wrote this story down in a book.

"Now," he thought, "people all over the world will know just how much God loves us all."

THE GREAT INVENTOR

KING UZZIAH WAS always busy inventing things. "No enemy will ever win while I rule in Jerusalem," he thought as he scrambled up onto the city walls.

"Workmen!" he shouted. "Build towers at every corner of these walls. I have invented giant catapults to hurl stones and arrows at any army that comes too near."

When he was tired of fighting Philistines and building castles, farming became his great hobby. He was quite sure he could do a better job than the farmers. So all over the land he grew wonderful fruit and vegetables and invented ways of breeding bigger and stronger animals.

Everyone had so much good food to eat, they told him what a great king he was.

"Yes, I am rather clever," he thought as he went into the temple one day. "God must be pleased to have a man like me as king."

As he sat there proudly, he noticed the priests hurrying about offering the peoples' presents to God and burning the sweet smelling incense. "I could invent much better ways of doing all that," he thought. "I'd better show those priests how to run this temple."

So he picked up the incense burner and pushed his way into the most holy part of the temple. God had said no one but the priests should ever go in there, because they knew exactly how he liked to be worshiped.

From every corner of the great temple the priests came running in horror. "Your Majesty!" they gasped. "Only the priests of Aaron's family can burn incense. Come out of the holy place at once; even we have to be specially chosen to go in there!"

"Whom do you think you're talking to!" demanded Uzziah proudly. "I'm the greatest king that there's ever been. I can do just as I like." But he was forgetting that God cannot bear proud people.

"Look!" gasped the priests, stepping back in amazement as they pointed at the king. Ugly, white patches were appearing all over his face. "Your Majesty has leprosy!" they cried.

No one with that dreadful illness was ever allowed in the temple, so the priests hustled Uzziah out of the back door. As soon as he realized what his pride had done to him, he ran away down the street crying.

Everyone was so frightened they would catch leprosy too that the king had to live in a house by himself for the rest of his life and no one ever went near him. His son ruled the land for him and King Uzziah's inventing days were over for ever.

THE MAN WHO KNEW THE SECRET

I CAN SEE GOD!" gasped a young man called Isaiah. He had come to pray in the temple and suddenly found himself looking right up into heaven. There was God himself sitting on a great throne with angels all about him. The whole temple seemed to shake and rumble and poor Isaiah was terrified.

"I have a message for my people," God said. "If they do not follow me and keep my rules they will be in dreadful danger. Their enemies will come and carry them away as slaves again, burn their houses and knock down this temple. Who will go and warn them of these terrible things?"

"Surely someone will offer," thought Isaiah. "This is dreadful." But no one in heaven said a word and the angels covered their faces with their wings.

"I'll go and tell them for you," Isaiah found himself saying.

From that moment he became God's special friend and God let Isaiah into his great secret. The young man could hardly believe his ears when he heard it.

"One day I am going to show people JUST what I am really like," said God. "A girl who is not married will have a baby. That special child will be my Son. He will be called the Mighty God, the Prince of Peace. He will tell you all about me."

"How shall we know when this great King is coming?" gasped Isaiah.

"Watch for a prophet shouting in the desert," replied God. "He will be just like Elijah and will tell you when to get ready."

Isaiah hurried off to share this great news, and everyone began to expect the person they called the Messiah to come any day. But it was seven hundred years before Jesus was born. People waited and hoped for him all that time.

God had something more to tell Isaiah, but this secret made him very sad. "When I send this man, people will laugh at him and they will not listen to what he says about me. They will hurt him and beat him, spit at him and pull out his hair. He will be sadder than any man has ever been. Then they will lead him away and kill him."

"No! No!" cried poor Isaiah. "This can't be right! Why won't you stop them from doing that?"

"Because it is all part of my plan," explained God. "No one keeps my rules all the time. Everyone does bad things. So none of you can come to heaven and be with me. You all deserve to die. But I am going to let your King be hurt and die instead of you. This will make a way for you to live forever with me in heaven."

"I don't understand," sobbed Isaiah. "That can't be fair."

"He will not stay dead," explained God. "I shall make him live again and he will be King of the whole world for ever."

No one could understand what Isaiah was talking about this time, so he wrote it all down very carefully. When Jesus died on the cross hundreds of years later, and then rose again, people read that book and suddenly realized just what it all meant.

THE EMPEROR WHO WAS RUDE TO GOD

PEOPLE WERE running into Jerusalem from all over the land. "Close the gates," they gasped, "the Assyrians are coming! Whatever shall we do?"

"Pray and trust in God," shouted their king Hezekiah as he stood on the steps of the temple with Isaiah beside him.

"But they are marching through the world," replied the frightened people, "burning cities and killing everyone inside. Their army is so big there is no hope for us. Perhaps we should have listened to Isaiah?"

For many years he had been warning the people, just as he promised God he would. He used to meet them at the temple door and say, "Here you come to pray, dressed up in your best, strutting like proud chickens. But God won't hear you while you are mean to poor people and cruel to children. You only pretend to be good. Say you're sorry and change, or you will all be slaves again."

Now the people realized just how much danger they were in, so they turned back to God very quickly indeed!

"Remember the Assyrians are only humans," shouted the king. "Now we have God on our side."

Emperor Sennacherib of Assyria was so cunning he sent three clever men on ahead of his army. "Frighten the people into opening their gates for us," he told them.

Thousands of faces peeped nervously over the city wall when the three men arrived and began to shout as loudly as they could. "Why don't you just give up?" they yelled. "You know you can't hold out against us for long. You are stuck in your city like birds in a cage. God can't help you. He has no power against the Emperor. Open the gates and we will give you wine and grapes and lots of bread and honey."

The people were all terribly hungry, but no one moved. They were trusting in God.

So the men tried a new trick and sent a letter to King Hezekiah. When he read it he began to feel really frightened.

"I have destroyed all the rest of the world. Now I am coming for you. God won't be able to do anything when I tunnel under your walls or batter down your gates."

Quickly Hezekiah ran into the temple and laid the frightening letter out before God. "What shall I do?" he prayed.

God's answer came at once through Isaiah. "Sennacherib has been rude to me, so I will show the whole world who I really am. Not one arrow shall be shot against Jerusalem, and I will take him back in shame to Nineveh like a bull with a ring in its nose."

It really looked as if Isaiah was not speaking the truth this time when the huge army appeared and camped all around the city. But that night the soldiers caught a dreadful illness, and by morning they all lay dead in their tents. Sennacherib was so embarrassed he stumbled back home and two of his sons stabbed him to death.

So the whole world saw how dangerous it is to be rude to God and they flocked to his temple to bring him presents.

THE NAUGHTIEST BOY WHO EVER LIVED

ONE DAY King Hezekiah was very ill, and a visit from Isaiah did NOT cheer him up. "I'm afraid God says you are going to die," the old prophet said sadly.

When he had gone, Hezekiah turned his face to the wall and cried bitterly. "Please God," he prayed, "make me well again."

God heard his voice and sent Isaiah hurrying back to the king's bedroom just a few minutes later. "In three days you will be better," smiled the old man, "and you will rule for another fifteen years."

It actually might have been better if Hezekiah had not lived longer, because of two things that happened in those extra fifteen years.

First, some very smart looking visitors arrived from a place called Babylon.

"You shall see our wonderful temple," smiled Hezekiah. But he just could not stop himself from showing off, so he took them into all the secret rooms where the wonderful treasures were hidden.

"Why ever did you let them see all that?" scolded Isaiah. "Didn't you see the way their greedy eyes gleamed? One day Babylon will come back and steal it all."

"Never," laughed Hezekiah. "Babylon is too far away." But he was wrong.

The other thing which happened in those fifteen years was the arrival of Hezekiah's son Manasseh.

He must have been the naughtiest boy who ever lived! He was in trouble as soon as he could crawl. Whatever his father wanted him to do, he always did the opposite!

When Manasseh was only twelve he became king, so no one could stop him from doing anything bad that he felt like doing. "My father loved God," he grinned. "But I think it would be far more fun to worship God's enemy, Satan."

Soon he had killed so many people that the streets of Jerusalem were stained red with blood. Witches and wizards were everywhere, and statues of Baal were even placed in God's temple.

The people were delighted. They were sick of the prophets telling them to be good. "Let's all be really bad instead," they chuckled. "We can do what we like without God." But they were wrong there.

God sent their enemies, the Assyrians, back to attack Jerusalem, allowing them to flood into the city and drag Manasseh away to Nineveh in chains.

In the dark, damp dungeon where he had been thrown, Manasseh cried as he remembered the days when he had been a little boy. "My father used to tell me how kind God is," he sobbed, "but I wonder if he could ever forgive someone as bad as I."

Of course God could, and he made the Assyrians send Manasseh home to be king once again.

It was hard for people to recognise Manasseh; he was so different. He rushed around the land burning the statues of Baal and chasing away the witches. But the people had learnt to be bad by then, and they were enjoying it!

They had forgotten Isaiah and what he said would happen to them if they did not keep God's rules.

THE LOST BOOK

GOOD!" SMILED the followers of Baal. "Our new king Josiah is only eight years old. Perhaps he will be as bad as his grandfather Manasseh was when he was a boy king."

But they could not have been more wrong. While he was still only a child, Josiah decided to love and follow God forever. How sad he used to feel when he looked at the crumbling old temple, which was almost falling down. "One day, when I grow up, I will rebuild it," he used to think.

But when all the workmen arrived the high priest was not pleased. "What a noise they make!" he muttered. "And now I'll have to tidy my storeroom so they can work in here tomorrow."

The little room was so full of rubbish it was hard to squeeze inside the door. Then, as he began pulling things off a high shelf, his fingers touched something very strange. "Whatever is this?" he wondered in amazement.

"It's terribly old," gasped his secretary. I think we should take it to the king."

"Your Majesty," they puffed as they ran into the palace, "we've found part of the old book of Moses."

Hundred of years before, when the people had first made their promise to God, Moses wrote a book. He put down God's rules and what would happen to the people if they did not keep them. Then he put the scrolls in the golden box called the ark.

"Every seven years," he told the priests, "you must take them out and read the book aloud to all the people." (In those days it was usually only the priests who could read.)

"But we haven't done that for years," the high priest told the king. "We didn't even know this book was lost. No wonder the people have broken their promise to God."

"This is terrible," said the king when the book was read to him. "All these dreadful things will soon be happening to us." He was so sad he was crying when he said to the high priest, "Please go and find out from God what we should do."

Isaiah was dead by then, but God had a woman called Huldah to speak for him. What she said made them all sadder than ever. "It is too late now. God says the people have turned against him in their hearts. All the dreadful things that are written in the scrolls of Moses will happen."

"Perhaps God will change his mind," thought the young king sadly. "Call everyone to the temple, old and young, rich and poor, and the book shall be read to them all."

For the rest of his life, Josiah worked hard to turn the people back to God again. But they only pretended to follow God. They still believed in Baal in their hearts. They went on being cruel to children who had no parents and mean to the people who had no money. Yet God still loved them enough to give them one last chance.

THE BOOK
THE KING BURNED

BEFORE BABY Jeremiah was even born, God had chosen him; and while he was still only a boy, God spoke to him for the very first time. "Go and tell my people this is their very last chance to turn back to me," he said.

"I can't be a prophet," stammered Jeremiah. "I'm too young; I wouldn't know what to say."

So God reached down from heaven and touched Jeremiah's lips. "I have put my words in your mouth," he said kindly.

Into the busy Jerusalem marketplace marched Jeremiah. "Listen!" he shouted above all the noise. "God says he loves you. He wants you to be happy. Remember how he always looks after us when we stay close to him. But all you ever do is turn your backs on him. He will have to destroy us and our city unless you change."

But no one would listen; they just turned away and went on laughing and talking.

So Jeremiah called to the children who were busy collecting firewood.

"We can't stop," they shouted back. "We're going to bake cakes and give them to the moon; she's queen of heaven, and our god now."

"No! No!" said Jeremiah in horror. "Don't you know GOD MADE THE MOON! He's the only one who can help you." But the children only laughed and ran away.

"Perhaps the priests in the temple will listen," thought Jeremiah, but they were furious when he told them God was sending a terrible enemy from the north to destroy their temple.

"He's telling lies," said the men who only pretended to be prophets. "God says he'll go on caring for his people whatever we do."

"They're making that up," shouted Jeremiah. But Pashhur the priest had him whipped and chained up all night outside the door of the temple. "Never come in here again," he threatened.

In the morning crowds of rude people gathered around to laugh at Jeremiah. "Nothing you say will ever really happen," they jeered.

When he was set free, Jeremiah walked away alone down a dark alley and he was so sad he cried. "No one will listen to me," he sobbed. "I won't say another word. I'll let God destroy them; they deserve it."

But God loved his people so much he said to Jeremiah, "Write down everything I told you in a book." That was extremely difficult, because Jeremiah could not write. So he asked his friend Baruch to help him do it.

"I'm not allowed in the temple," said Jeremiah when they had finished at last. "You go there and read my book aloud."

"They've taken it to the king!" said Baruch when he came back full of excitement.

"Wonderful!" exclaimed Jeremiah. "When the lost book of Moses was read to the king's father, Josiah, he cried and spent the rest of his life turning the people back to God."

But this king was not good like Josiah. He sat in his palace, which he had painted bright red, and roared with laughter at Jeremiah's book. Then he cut it up with his knife and threw it into the fire.

Poor Jeremiah was flung into prison, and everyone seemed to forget him. But God remembered he was there, and he still had a job for his prophet to do.

WHEN THE GREAT PLAN NEARLY FAILED

GOD LOOKED DOWN at the great King Nebuchadnezzar of Babylon and thought sadly, "I will have to allow him to punish my people. They will not listen to Jeremiah."

Nebuchadnezzar was determined to rule the whole world and thought he was the cleverest man who ever lived. He never guessed that he was only part of God's plan.

"I hear that the temple in Jerusalem is full of wonderful treasure," he said. "We will go there and take it." So off he marched with his army and they surrounded the walls of Jerusalem, just as Jeremiah had said that they would.

"What shall we do?" panicked the king of Judah. "Where's that man Jeremiah? He might pray for us." So he sent Pashhur the priest to bring Jeremiah out of prison.

"God saved us before when our city was in danger," said the king. "What does he tell us to do now?"

"He says open the gates and give yourselves up," replied Jeremiah, "because you're not really sorry for all you have done."

Pashhur the priest was furious. "You're just making that up to frighten us all," he thundered and, dragging Jeremiah back to prison, he threw him down a deep, well.

"I shall die now," thought poor Jeremiah as he sank into the slimy mud at the bottom. But God was still taking care of him, and a kind African man who worked in the prison hauled him out on a long rope. Then the man went to the king. "It's not fair to treat Jeremiah like this," he said bravely.

The king had a nasty feeling Jeremiah might have been right all the time, so he replied, "Let him live in the prison garden and feed him well, but don't tell the priests."

One terrible day, Nebuchadnezzar managed to knock down and flatten the walls of Jerusalem and into the city he marched. All the beautiful houses and palaces were burned, the treasure was stolen and, worst of all, Solomon's golden temple was knocked down into a heap of blackened stones.

"Everyone who is good at anything will come back to Babylon and work for us," said King Nebuchadnezzar. "We'll take all the builders, carpenters, jewelery makers and writers. All the cooks, singers and dancers. The beautiful women and strong, young men will all be ours. Only the ill and the old and the poor will be left behind."

Away the people went, dragged off as slaves once again, and Jeremiah was left alone in the empty, ruined city. He spent his time wandering among the stones, praying for the people who had gone so far away.

Satan really thought he had finished off God's plans completely this time, but once again he was wrong.

Suddenly, one day, God spoke again to Jeremiah. "Write a letter and send it to all the slaves in Babylon," he said. "They are crying and asking me for help. Tell them I still love them, and in seventy years their children shall return and build Jerusalem again. Remind my people that one day their Messiah will come and show people how to live forever."

When Jeremiah had sent off that letter, he died a happier man.

THE FOUR PRINCES

THE DESERT SAND was burning hot and the chains dug painfully into their wrists. Those poor slaves were dragged for hundreds of miles until they were so tired they could hardly stand.

The children, who had once made cakes for the moon, cried bitterly as they longed for their homes. Many of them lost their parents in the crowd or saw them being killed by the cruel soldiers.

In the long line of slaves were four young princes. They were only boys, but they tried to march along bravely, remembering that they were still members of the royal family.

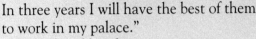

"Whatever happens to us," said Daniel, the oldest, "we four will stay close to God and keep all his rules."

"Yes," the others agreed. "We'll be like our uncle, good King Josiah."

When they reached the palace in Babylon they could hardly believe their eyes. "This must be the most beautiful place in the world," they gasped as they looked at all the flowers which hung from baskets everywhere.

"These Jews are clever people," said King Nebuchadnezzar, stroking his black beard. "If I am to rule the world I need people like them to help me with my office work." Turning to his servant, Ashpenaz, he said, "Pick out the strongest and brightest boys from among these slaves and teach them to read and write our language. In three years I will have the best of them to work in my palace."

Daniel and his three cousins were delighted when they were chosen to go to this new school. "Life in Babylon might not be so bad after all," they thought.

But when they filed into the school dining room for the first meal they began to feel worried. "Whatever shall we do?" whispered Daniel. "This is the kind of food God told us not to eat."

"We promised we would always keep his rules," said the others doubtfully, "but, if we do, we might be thrown out of the school."

Just then Ashpenaz saw them whispering. "Eat up quickly!" he said crossly. "You are very lucky boys; this food and wine comes from the king's own kitchen."

"Please sir," gulped Daniel, "my cousins and I are sorry, but our God doesn't like us to eat some kinds of meat."

"If you start looking pale and thin," shouted Ashpenaz, "the king will cut my head off."

"Please sir," pleaded Daniel, "try us on vegetables and water just for ten days."

It was more than a week later when Ashpenaz noticed the four princes again. "You look so rosy and well," he smiled, "that you can eat whatever you like."

It was not much fun living on vegetables for three years, but God helped the princes with their school work and they learned faster than any of the other boys.

Finally the time came for them all to be brought to the king. The great examination took all day and the questions were very difficult. Each boy hoped he would be chosen as one of the king's wise men.

At last Nebuchadnezzar was ready to announce the winners. "I'll have those four," he said. "They are ten times better than anyone else," and he pointed straight at the four princes who kept God's rules.

THE NIGHTMARE

KING NEBUCHADNEZZAR sat up in bed and screamed. "I've had a dreadful dream," he yelled at his sleepy servants. "Fetch all my wise men here at once."

Footsteps rang all over the palace, but no one bothered to wake the four Jewish princes.

"Tell me what my dream means," demanded the king as all the cleverest men in Babylon crowded into his bedroom.

When they did not know he flew into a terrible rage. "Guards," he screamed. "Take them all away and kill them."

"You four must die as well," said the soldiers as they marched into the princes' room and pulled them out of bed.

"Please ask the king to give us more time," protested Daniel. "Then we can ask the one real God the meaning of this dream."

"You can have until tomorrow," growled the king, "but not one minute more."

So the princes prayed all night long until God told Daniel the meaning of the dream.

"Well?" demanded Nebuchadnezzar when they were shown into his throne room next day. "Can you understand dreams?"

"No," replied Daniel, "but God knows everything and he has shown me what to tell you. Your Majesty dreamed about a great golden statue."

"Yes!" exclaimed the king.

"Then a stone rolled down from the mountains and knocked it into pieces," continued the prince.

"Yes, yes," said the king, "but what does it MEAN?"

"You are the golden statue," replied Daniel, "the greatest king in the world. But one day, many years from now, God will send a King who does not look very important, but he will rule the world for ever."

"You are the cleverest man in the land," shouted Nebuchadnezzar. "You and your cousins shall help me rule all Babylon."

It looked as if everything was going well for them now, but there was more trouble to come.

"I will make a statue like the one in my dream," thought Nebuchadnezzar as he climbed into bed that night. "It will be the biggest in the world and everyone shall bow down to it."

He was delighted when the great model was finished, because he thought it looked rather like himself. "Call all the most important people in the world to come here to Babylon," he ordered. "And when the band begins to play they shall all bow down together."

"Whatever are we going to do?" said the cousins as they stood among the huge crowd waiting for the music to begin. "We would be breaking God's rules if we bowed to that statue. But we're sure to be killed if we don't."

Daniel was not with them that day, but they did not need to ask him; they knew what they should do.

As the music of the band began to blare out across the plain, everyone bowed until their heads touched the ground. But three men were left standing straight and tall.

"What will happen to us now?" they whispered as they heard an angry roar from the throne where the king was sitting.

"You're in serious trouble!" said the soldiers as they seized the three princes and began to pull them off towards Nebuchadnezzar.

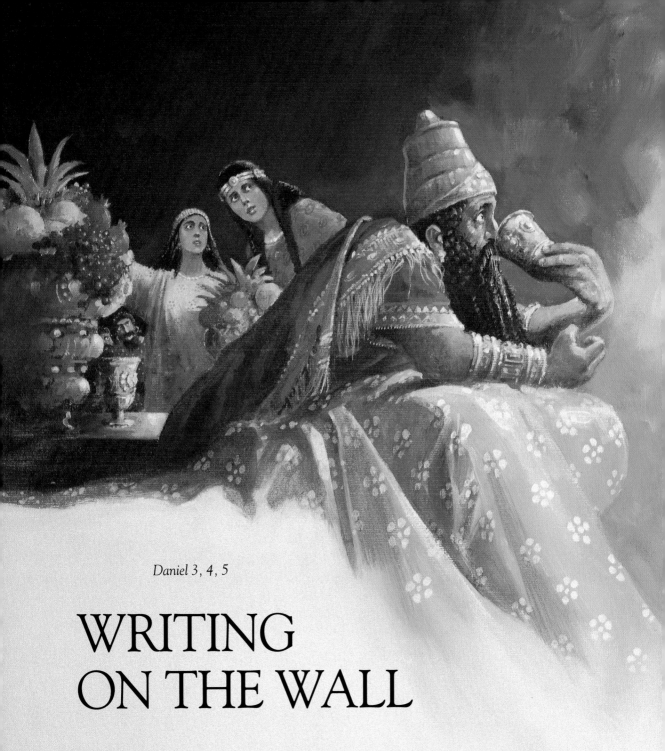

Daniel 3, 4, 5

WRITING
ON THE WALL

H OW DARE YOU!" roared the king
when he caught sight of the Jewish
princes standing upright in the
middle of a sea of bowing people.
"Either you worship my statue like
everyone else or I shall have you flung in
the fire. No God can save you from me."

"Our God can," replied the princes, "but
even if we have to die, we shall never bow
down to any other God but him."

"Burn them!" yelled the king, quite
beside himself with rage.

The workmen who had made the great
statue had used very hot fires called furnaces

מְנֵא מְנֵא

to melt down all the gold. Their heat was so terrific that the soldiers who threw in the princes shriveled up and died.

The king sat biting his fingers with rage as he sat watching the furnace. Then, suddenly, his face changed from anger to fear. "Look!" he pointed with a trembling finger. "Those men are still walking about in the flames, and there's someone in there with them who looks like God himself."

When the princes stepped out of the fire their clothes were not even singed.

"Your God is the King of all gods," gasped Nebuchadnezzar, and for the rest of his life the four Jewish princes were the most important men in Babylon.

But things were very different when his son Belshazzar became king. He did not like Jews, so he sent them away from the palace.

"Let's have a party," he giggled one day. "We'll ask a thousand guests."

"But Your Majesty," protested his wise men, "our enemies the Persians are marching towards Babylon."

"Our city walls are thicker than any in the world," laughed Belshazzar. "They'll never get in here."

Lights, music and laughter filled the palace that night, and the king and his friends were too busy enjoying themselves to notice enemy soldiers digging a secret passage under the walls of Babylon.

"Go and fetch all those golden cups my father took from the temple in Jerusalem," hiccuped Belshazzar. "We'll use them to drink to the health of all our gods."

God was furious when he saw what they were doing with his beautiful golden goblets and suddenly the noise of the party died away into an uncomfortable silence.

"What's that?" gasped the king, turning white with fear. "I see a giant hand writing on the wall."

No one could read the strange words that flickered in the candlelight, and everyone was frightened.

"Your father used to have a wise man called Daniel," said Belshazzar's mother. "Perhaps he could help."

"F-f-f-fetch him!" stuttered the king, and he shivered with fright until Daniel arrived in the palace.

"That message was written by God," Daniel told him. "He says you are no longer fit to be king."

Not many hours later enemy soldiers crept into the city. The Persians had captured Babylon, and before morning Belshazzar was dead.

INTO THE LIONS' DEN

THREE MEN CROUCHED in the bushes at the bottom of Daniel's garden. "There he is," they whispered, "praying again! We'll soon be rid of him now!"

Daniel knelt down by the open window of his bedroom. Three times every day he prayed there as he looked out towards Jerusalem. He did not care that a law had been passed in the land to say no one was allowed to pray for a whole month.

As he knelt there that day, praying for Jerusalem, he tried to remember how it had looked. It was so many years since he had been there, and tears began to run down his cheeks. "Please God, forgive your people the Jews," he sobbed. "We are so sorry we turned away from you. Please let us go back and rebuild our land."

Just then a wonderful thing happened. The angel Gabriel himself suddenly appeared beside him, but only Daniel knew he was there.

"God loves you," he said, "and he hears your prayer. Soon Jerusalem will be rebuilt, and not long after that God will send his Messiah. But when men kill him unfairly, Jerusalem will have to be destroyed once again."

Daniel bowed his head and thought about this strange message, but he never realized his enemies were still watching him.

The new King Darius liked Daniel very much and he had made him very important again. That made other men so jealous, they began looking for ways to get Daniel into trouble.

"You are so great," they said to the king, "you should show everyone you are as powerful as any god. Make a rule that no one prays except to you for a whole month.

If they do, have them thrown into a pit full of hungry lions."

The king felt most flattered, but he did not realize they were only trying to trap their enemy. They knew Daniel would take no notice of this rule and would go on praying three times a day, just like he always had.

"We've got you now!" they snickered from their hiding place in the garden. "Let's go and tell the king!"

Darius was terribly upset. "However will I manage without Daniel," he wondered. All day long he tried to think of a way to save his friend, but Persian laws could never be changed, not even by the king. So in the evening soldiers came and threw Daniel down into the pit of lions.

"May your God keep you safe!" shouted the king as he watched Daniel disappear. Sadly he trailed home to his palace and went to bed without his supper. All night long he tossed and turned, worrying about poor Daniel. Could his God save him? He had once saved those three men in the fire, but he shook his head sadly when he thought about those fierce lions.

As soon as it was light, he hurried to the lions' pit and had the heavy, stone door moved away. "Daniel," he called, "has your God saved you?"

"Yes, Your Majesty," came Daniel's voice from far below. "His angel shut the mouths of the lions."

Darius was so delighted he had Daniel pulled out at once and his enemies were thrown into the pit instead. The lions tore them to pieces before they even reached the ground!

From that day King Darius believed in God for the rest of his life.

HOME AGAIN

THE NEW KING CYRUS leaned back in his chair and smiled at the old man sitting beside him. "Daniel," he said, "I love to hear your stories about God. Tell me what Jerusalem is really like."

But tears were running down old Daniel's face and he could hardly speak. "Jerusalem has been burnt, and the temple is flattened," he sighed. "We Jews always cry when we remember it. When we have a holiday, we sit by the rivers of Babylon and we try to sing songs to God. Sometimes we cry so much, we have to stop singing and put our harps away."

"That's terrible," said the king, jumping to his feet. "God will be angry with me if I let his house lie in ruins. I will send the Jews back home and pay for a new temple. I'll even let you have all God's treasure back."

When the slaves heard the news they were so happy they thought they must be dreaming.

The long line of people stretched for miles. There were thousands of people walking along that road, pulling handcarts piled high with possessions. Behind them plodded the camels and donkeys with the temple gold loaded on their backs.

They were so happy they sang all the way, but when they finally reached Jerusalem their songs died away into a sad silence. "However will we build all this again?" they whispered miserably.

"It's just a heap of blackened stones," said the children, and the old people began to search about trying to find where their homes might once have been.

"The temple used to stand here," shouted their chief priest. "We could still offer God the presents we brought him, here, in the open air."

Everyone began to cheer up then. Soon they were singing so loudly, the noise echoed in the hills and valleys around the city, and that is when their trouble began!

Other people called Samaritans were living in the land by then and they were furious. "We don't want these Jews back here," they said, storming into Jerusalem.

The people had begun to build their new temple while the priests sang them songs about God, but the angry Samaritans frightened them all so much they quickly put away their tools. They quite forgot to ask God to help them, which made him very sad.

A year later two prophets walked into the tumbledown city and looked about in disgust. "All you think about are houses for yourselves," shouted one of them, whose name was Haggai. "But God's temple is still in ruins."

"You should be getting Jerusalem ready for your Messiah," put in the other prophet Zechariah. "One day he'll come riding in on a donkey."

All the people were so excited to hear about this they began to build again at once, and the Samaritans actually left them alone—for a while.

But Satan must have heard about the Messiah too, and he was really worried. "I don't want God showing people how to live forever," he hissed. "And I don't want him suddenly appearing in Jerusalem on a donkey. It's time I thought of a way to kill all the Jews in the world, once and for all."

And he very nearly managed it!

THE MOST BEAUTIFUL GIRL IN THE WORLD

NO! I WON'T GO! Let me stay with uncle Mordecai." The tears were streaming down Esther's cheeks as the king's servants tried to drag her away to the palace.

Instead of going back to Jerusalem with the other Jews, Esther's uncle had stayed behind to look after her when her parents died. Perhaps Esther and her uncle would have traveled to Jerusalem when she was older, but all their plans went wrong when the king had a dreadful fight with his wife.

"I'll send my servants out to look for the prettiest girl in the world," shouted the king, "and she'll be queen instead of you."

Hundreds of lovely girls were delighted to be chosen to take part in the great competition, but when the king's men noticed Esther's great beauty, she was not pleased at all.

"You'll have to go to the king," whispered her uncle sadly, "but don't tell him you're a Jew. Just remember God is with you."

Esther was so very beautiful the king fell in love with her at once, and the whole country was given a holiday on their wedding day. But the new queen missed her uncle terribly. She was never allowed to speak to him again, but every day he came to the palace gate and waved up at her window.

While Mordecai was standing there, Haman, the prime minister, used to ride in to see the king. He was so important everyone bowed to the ground, but not Mordecai! "Why doesn't that stupid man ever bow to me?" snapped Haman one day.

"Because he is a Jew, my lord," answered the servants. "His people bow only to God."

"I'll make them all sorry for that," roared Haman as Satan put a wicked idea into his head.

"Your Majesty," said Haman next day, "there are some very bad people called Jews scattered all over the kingdom. I think it would be safer to have them all killed."

"Do whatever you like," yawned the king. So Haman sat down and wrote out this order: "On the thirteenth day of the last month of this year, every Jew is to die."

The news spread to every Jewish home in the world, and the people who were building the new temple in Jerusalem were horrified.

Queen Esther looked anxiously out of her window. Whatever was the matter with her uncle? "Go down and ask him why he looks so sad," she told one of her servants, and soon she too heard the dreadful news.

"Your uncle wants you to go to ask the king for help," added the servant.

"But I can't do that," cried Esther. "Go back and tell him no one can see the king unless he sends for them. They would be killed if they did, and he has not called me for over a month now."

She waited nervously until the servant came back, but the secret message he whispered in her ear made her shake with fear. "Have you forgotten you are also a Jew? You will have to die with the rest of us. Yet perhaps God made you queen so you could save us all."

"Tell my uncle that I will go to the king," gasped Esther, "but all the Jews must pray for me."

THE BRAVE QUEEN

QUEEN ESTHER walked slowly towards the throne room with a wildly beating heart.
"You can't go in there," gasped the servants. "The king didn't ask for you."
Even though she knew she might be killed, Esther walked straight past them and up towards the golden throne.

As the king looked up crossly from the papers he was reading he noticed how very beautiful Esther was and he forgave her at once.

"I want to give a party for you tonight," she said. "Will you come and bring Prime Minister Haman?"

"Certainly," smiled the king.

Haman was also terribly pleased when he heard he had been invited to the queen's private party, and he rode home to change his suit in a very good mood. But suddenly all his happiness turned into rage. "That Jew still won't bow to me!" he growled to his wife. "Tomorrow I will ask the king if I can have him hanged at once."

"That WAS lovely!" smiled the king when Esther's party was over. "What can I give you as a present?"

Here was her chance! But poor Esther was so nervous all she could say was, "Please come back for another party tomorrow."

Perhaps the king had eaten too much, because he couldn't sleep that night. "Read to me," he ordered one of his servants, "until I fall asleep."

But the story he heard made him sit up in bed in surprise. Two men had once tried to kill him, and a Jew called Mordecai had saved his life. "What reward did I give him for that?" he asked the servant.

"None, Your Majesty," was the reply.

"I must do something about that," thought the king.

In the morning Haman came hurrying to the palace to ask the king to hang Mordecai.

"You're just the man I want," smiled the king. "What shall I do for someone who has really pleased me?"

Haman was sure HE must be the man the king wanted to reward, and he thought, "I'll use this chance to get rid of Mordecai." So, with a cunning smile he said, "Your Majesty, I'd put the man on your finest horse and have him led through the city. Anyone who did not bow to him should be hanged."

"Good," said the king. "Go and do all that to Mordecai, and you can lead the horse."

Poor Haman. He was cross!

The queen's party went so well that evening that the king leaned over the dinner table and said, "There MUST be something I can do for you, my queen."

Esther took a very deep breath and remembered all the Jews who were praying for her. "Please let me live," she managed to say. "A wicked man is planning to kill me and all my people by the end of the year."

"WHO IS HE?" demanded the king angrily.

"He is sitting there!" said Esther, pointing at Haman.

Next day it was not Mordecai who was hanged but Haman, and soon the king had made Esther's uncle the new prime minister.

So all the Jews in the kingdom were saved because one pretty girl was part of God's plan.

JERUSALEM IN DANGER

THE RUINS OF Jerusalem looked ghostly and sad in the moonlight as the little donkey picked a path through the fallen stones.

Nehemiah shuddered as he rode along thinking about all the treasure lying in the new temple. How easily an enemy could creep up in the darkness and steal it all away once more. "I won't feel happy until I see high walls around this city again," he thought, "and streets and shops where only owls and bats live now."

He had only just arrived from Persia where he had been working for the king. One day his brother had arrived at the palace, bringing terrible news from Jerusalem. "Our city is still in ruins around the new temple, but we are all too frightened of the Samaritans to go on building," his brother had said. So Nehemiah had come to see if he could help.

"Let's start work at once," he said to the frightened people the next day.

"What about the Samaritans?" they gasped.

"God's stronger than they are!" smiled Nehemiah.

But they had hardly begun to build when along came Sanballat and Tobiah, the leaders of the Samaritans, and how they laughed when they saw what was happening. "A few miserable Jews can't possibly rebuild a great city," grinned Sanballat.

"Why, even a fox could knock that wall down with its tail," added Tobiah.

Nehemiah said nothing, but under his breath he prayed quietly.

As the walls grew higher the Samaritans soon stopped laughing. "This could be serious," they muttered. "We must band ourselves together into an army and attack before this wall is finished."

"What shall we do?" gasped the terrified Jews. "They're hiding in the hills sharpening their arrows."

"Don't worry!" shouted Nehemiah. "Just remember how great God is! He'll help us to finish the walls before they arrive."

He gave everyone a weapon and added, "Don't stop work; just keep a sword in your belt and a spear close at hand. But if you hear my trumpet, fight for your lives."

From dawn until the stars came out again everybody worked together, singing all the time. Even the children carried buckets of water, while their mothers mixed cement. No one dared take their clothes off at night, and their swords were always beside them.

"They're too strong for us," muttered the Samaritans as they watched the walls grow higher every day. "We must frighten Nehemiah away."

The next day an old prophet shuffled up to Jerusalem. "I have a message from God for you," he told Nehemiah. "He says you're in great danger! Run quickly and hide in the temple."

Nehemiah stared hard at the old man and then he said, "God would never tell me to run away. Sanballat and Tobiah paid you to frighten me, didn't they?" The lying prophet turned very red and hurried away.

One day, the enemy soldiers heard a strange sound. As they crept nearer to the city they saw to their amazement that the walls were finished already. Around the top marched all the Jews, singing to God at the tops of their voices while the bands played and the children clapped. "We're too late!" they raged. "Their God has won."

THE PARTY THAT LASTED A WEEK

NEHEMIAH WAS SO horrified, he could hardly believe his eyes. He had been back in Persia, working for the king once again; but as soon as he arrived in Jerusalem he realized something had gone very wrong.

"This is the Sabbath day," he thought, "yet people are working in the wine factories and all the shops are open. Don't they remember that God wanted this day to be a time to rest and enjoy their families?"

Everywhere he went in that brand new city he saw people breaking God's rules once again and being selfish, mean and cruel.

"How could they treat God like this, when he has done so much for them?" Nehemiah said to his friend Ezra. "Everything will go wrong again if they go on disobeying him."

"The trouble is," replied Ezra, "the people don't even know God's law. They've been away as slaves for so long, they haven't had the old books of Moses read to them."

"Then we'll read them in the temple at once," said Nehemiah.

"This must be the wettest day since Noah's flood," shivered the people as they huddled in the temple yard. The rain beat on their heads and trickled down their necks, but their teeth chattered more with fear than with the cold.

Ezra was reading aloud to them all as he sat on a high, wooden stage, but the further he read the more miserable the people became. "What shall we do?" they cried. "We haven't been living the way God would like."

Ezra stopped and put the scrolls away. "Go home and get dry and warm," he said kindly. "Soon everyone shall have a week's holiday when something very special will happen."

From all over the world Jews were coming to Jerusalem. Thousands of people squashed inside the new city walls and camped in the streets and gardens. They had come for a party that would last a whole week and they were happier than

they had been in all their lives. The new Jerusalem was full of singing and dancing, lovely food and happy laughter.

"God wants us to be happy," Ezra told them. "His joy will give us strength to live HIS way."

All day long they listened to the Bible being read aloud. In little groups they talked about God and all he had done for them, or went into the temple to pray.

When a new prophet called Malachi began to speak, people clustered round him eagerly. "God wants you to know how much he loves you," he told them. "He is like the sun rising and shining on you warmly. He will open the windows of heaven and pour out on you all kinds of good things if you keep your promise to him. Make yourselves ready, because God himself is going to appear; the one you have been looking for will suddenly come here to this new temple."

So the people told God how sorry they were for breaking their promise and settled down to try and keep his rules while they waited eagerly for their Messiah.

They were all sure they would recognize him when he came; but did they?

EXCITEMENT IN HEAVEN

THE EXCITEMENT in heaven was so great that all the angels were talking at once. The time had come at last for the most important part of God's plan. He was actually going to send his Son down to live on earth so that people would know what God was really like.

"He's going to wear a man's body!" gasped the angels. "And begin as a baby, just like other people."

"God will have to choose a very special girl to be the mother," they added. "She'll probably be a princess."

The angels were wrong! God did not choose anyone rich or important for this special job. He picked a very ordinary country girl who was busy getting ready to marry the village carpenter. Her name was Mary, and one day, as she sat sewing her wedding dress, Gabriel, the most important angel in heaven, was sent by God to speak to her.

Mary was very frightened when she looked up and saw him smiling down at her.

"He's an angel!" she thought, and the wedding dress slipped to the floor.

"Mary," said Gabriel gently, "God loves you so much, he has chosen you to be the mother of his own Son." That made Mary feel even more frightened.

"How could I be the mother of God?" she thought. "I'm no one special."

"Don't be frightened," Gabriel went on. "God says that soon you will have a baby boy and you will call him Jesus. He is going to be King for ever and ever."

Mary was trembling so much she could hardly kneel on the floor. Ever since she had been tiny she had heard about this wonderful baby that God had promised to send one day, and every little girl secretly hoped that she might be chosen to be his mother. But Mary was still worried.

"How can I have a baby?" she stammered. "I'm not even married yet."

"God himself will be the Father of this Child," replied the angel simply.

All Mary's hopes and dreams seemed suddenly to be spoiled. For months now she and Joseph had been planning their little home behind the carpenter's shop. They were always talking about the babies they would have and how happy they would all be together. Perhaps she would not be able to marry Joseph now that she was going to be part of God's plan.

Gabriel was waiting quietly for her answer. Whatever should she say?

She realized that she loved God more than anything else, even more than Joseph, and bowing her head she whispered, "I am God's servant. I will do just as he says."

All the angels in heaven must have sighed with relief, but Gabriel knew something was still troubling her, so he said, "If you go and see your cousin Elizabeth, you will know that nothing is ever too difficult for God. She is a very old lady, but she too is going to have a baby son."

JOSEPH IS VERY WORRIED

PERHAPS I IMAGINED it all," thought Mary as she trudged along the dusty road. "I'm certainly not going to tell Joseph anything until I KNOW that what the angel said was true."

The only way to know for SURE was to go and see her cousin Elizabeth. So, very early that morning she had set off to walk to the old lady's house in the hills.

"Elizabeth is more like a grandmother than a cousin," thought Mary. "She's far too old to have a baby." But as soon as Mary walked into her cousin's home that evening, she saw that the angel had been speaking the truth. She stood still in the doorway gazing in astonishment at what she saw.

"All our lives we have longed for a son," Elizabeth told her later as they sat together in the evening shadows. "We had given up all hope, when suddenly an angel appeared to my husband and told him God was giving us a very special child. When he grows up his job will be to tell all the Jews in Israel that their promised King is coming at last."

Mary took a deep breath. She longed to tell Elizabeth that she had seen an angel too, but before she could speak the old lady's eyes filled with tears of joy. "It is a great honor for me to have you in my house," she whispered, "because I know your secret. You are going to be the mother of that King, God's very own Son."

Then Mary knew for certain that she had not imagined anything, so she stayed with Elizabeth for a few months until she could feel her own baby beginning to grow deep inside her.

Nervously, Mary pushed open the door of the carpenter's shop. She had missed Joseph so badly, but would he still love her when she told him the news?

"I just don't believe you," he gasped when she finally finished the story. "I can't possibly marry you if you are having someone else's baby." And he turned his back on her.

Poor Mary ran home crying through the dark streets, and Joseph paced up and down kicking miserably at the piles of sawdust. In those days if a girl had a baby when she was not married, everyone in the village threw stones at her until she died.

Joseph could not bear that to happen to Mary, because he loved her; yet why was she telling him lies? "Whatever shall I do?" he moaned as he flung himself down on his sleeping mat.

But when he was asleep, God sent an angel down into the carpenter's shop, and in a dream he spoke to Joseph. "Don't be frightened to marry Mary," the angel said kindly. "For she is speaking the truth. Call her baby 'Jesus', because he will save people from death and make it possible for them to be God's friends."

It was not even light when Joseph ran to Mary's house and soon they were hugging each other, breathless with excitement and joy. "We'll be married immediately," said Joseph. "Then I can help you keep God's special secret."

RUINED PLANS

TRAMP, TRAMP, TRAMP went the heavy shoes of the Roman soldiers as they marched into the village. People scattered in all directions and Joseph looked out of his carpenter's shop. "What do the Romans want now?" he wondered. Once again an enemy had marched into the land, but this time they did not steal the people away. They just made everyone do as they were told and pay them a lot of their money. The Jews were so miserable they were praying every day that God would send them their Messiah.

"I have a message for you all from the Emperor in Rome," shouted the officer in his shiny helmet. "Everyone must go back to the town where they were born so we can take a census."

"And make us pay more money," added Joseph crossly as he hurried into the little house behind the shop.

Mary was busy sewing baby clothes. How happy she felt as she looked round her little home. Everything was clean and ready, and soon the special baby would be lying safely in the cradle Joseph had made for him.

"I'm sorry," said Joseph sadly, "I'm afraid we shall have to travel to Bethlehem at once."

"But that's so far away!" exclaimed Mary. "I don't want the baby to be born among strangers."

"We have no choice," replied Joseph. "We must obey the Romans or they'll probably kill us."

"How much farther is Bethlehem?" whispered Mary three days later. "We must get there soon; the baby will be born tonight!"

"Look!" replied Joseph. "There, at the top of this hill. Those twinkling lights are Bethlehem. We'll soon have you in a quiet room and a comfortable bed."

They were cold, tired and very hungry, but as their little donkey began to pick his way up the steep path, Mary said suddenly, "We should have remembered! God's book says his Messiah will be born in Bethlehem."

"Yes," replied Joseph, smiling in the darkness, "God knew what he was doing all the time."

But it was very hard to remember that when they reached Bethlehem. The streets, houses and inns were crammed with everyone who had been forced to go back to Bethlehem to be registered. They all wanted to find somewhere to sleep and no one would make room for a dusty couple with no money. "Go away," they said roughly. "There's no room here for people like you."

"Help us!" pleaded Joseph. "My wife is having her baby; she must lie down."

Bang! went the doors as they were slammed in his face, and people turned their backs and hurried off to help the rich people.

No one seemed to care what happened to Mary and Joseph, and so, feeling terribly hungry and alone, they crept into the shelter of a tumbledown stable.

VISITORS IN THE NIGHT

WELL, IT'S BETTER than the street," said Mary, trying hard to smile as they looked around the stable in the flickering lamplight. HOW they longed for their own, clean, little house in Nazareth.

Sleepily the many camels and donkeys blinked at them. Chickens pecked around the floor and rats scuffled in the hay, but it was there that the King of all kings was born that night.

Carefully Mary wrapped him in strips of rag, and Joseph laid him in a manger full of hay. "Kings are usually born in grand palaces," he said, looking down at the sleeping baby. "I wonder why God allowed his Son to be born in a smelly place like this."

"Perhaps," smiled Mary, "it's just another part of God's secret. A way of showing poor, hungry, unwanted people just how much he loves them."

In Bethlehem that night people were too busy quarreling over beds and food to look up at the sky. But out in the fields the shepherds looked up at the stars as they guarded their sheep.

In those days people used to laugh at shepherds and call them rude names. No one wanted them in town. "They smell horrid!" everyone said.

Yet God must have thought they were very special. Suddenly, above the sigh of the wind in the olive trees, the shepherds heard a strange, unearthly sound. A beautiful, soft light began to fill the whole sky and there, beside them, stood an angel. They had never been so terrified in their lives!

"I am here to bring you wonderful news," the angel said. "Tonight in Bethlehem a King has just been born. If you want to find him, look in a hay manger."

As their eyes became used to the light, the shepherds saw that all around them were millions of gloriously colored angels, floating about and singing among the clouds.

"We never saw anything like this!" they muttered as the music and colors began to fade behind the stars. "And whoever heard of a King sleeping in a manger? We'd better go into town and see what's happening."

How surprised all the people in Bethlehem must have been to see a group of ragged shepherds pushing their way through the streets and peering into every barn and shed. "Where's the baby King?" they kept on asking, and how the people must have laughed at them!

At last they found their way into the rickety stable where Mary and Joseph were resting. "This MUST be the right place," they whispered. "Look! A newborn baby, cuddled up in the hay!" And shyly they knelt down on the dirty floor.

A crowd of curious people had followed them, and they all listened as the excited shepherds whispered their strange story. Everyone was amazed at what they said, but Mary and Joseph only smiled, because they already knew the secret.

THE EVIL PLAN

BABY!" ROARED King Herod furiously. "There's no baby in this palace. Tell them to go away."

"But Your Majesty," protested his servants, "these wise men have traveled hundreds of miles because they saw a brilliant new star in the east. They say it means our great King has been born at last!"

Herod jumped off his throne in horror. "I'm the king here!" he growled jealously. "Where do the old books say the Messiah will be born?"

"In the village of Bethlehem," his servants replied.

"Good," said Herod with a nasty smile. "Send those visitors in here to me."

"Naturally you would expect to find a baby king in a palace," he said as the wise men bowed low. "But listen," he added quietly, when all his servants had left, "Bethlehem is where you must look for this child. I too would like to worship him, so come back and tell me just where he is."

"They actually believed me!" cackled the wicked king as he stood at his window watching the wise men climbing back on to the camels. "No baby is having my crown!"

God's old enemy Satan was smiling too. He had been desperately trying to think of a way to get rid of Jesus, and now he realized Herod could do it for him.

As the wise men rode out of the city it was beginning to get dark, and suddenly, there in the sky, they saw the wonderful star they had seen back in their own land. "It's actually moving," they gasped. "It's leading us right to the new King."

Mary and Joseph were astonished when in through their little door squeezed so many rich and clever looking men. "We

come from the east to bring you these precious gifts," they said as they knelt down before the tiny baby."

"These men must know the secret," thought Mary. "Such beautiful presents are fit only for a king."

"Tomorrow we are going back to Jerusalem," smiled the wise men. "Herod also wants to come here and worship the child." But God knew just what Herod and Satan were planning, and that night his angel told the wise men in a dream not to go near the king.

When Herod realized he had been tricked he shook with rage. Calling his soldiers he gave them a terrible order. "Go secretly to Bethlehem," he whispered, "and kill every single baby boy!"

As the soldiers marched off through the night, Joseph was sleeping beside Mary having a dream. "Quick, Mary!" he gasped as he jumped out of bed in the darkness. "God has sent an angel to tell me Jesus is in great danger; we must escape at once."

The boots of the marching soldiers could almost be heard in the distance as the little family slipped out of the town and disappeared into the night.

"Can we go back to our own little home?" asked Mary hopefully.

"No," replied Joseph sadly. "We must run right away if we want to be safe from the king."

Herod thought he had won as he leaned back in his throne and sighed with relief, but all the time Jesus was growing up safely, far away in the land of Egypt.

It was not until after Herod had died that the little family traveled home to the carpenter's shop in Nazareth.

LOST!

FOR THE REST OF their lives Mary and Joseph never forgot the awful day when they lost Jesus. It happened while they were spending a holiday in Jerusalem. Everyone in Nazareth had locked up their shops and houses and the whole village had set off together for the great feast. Once a year the Jews all liked to go to the temple so they could talk to God and give him presents.

Mary and Joseph were so happy as they walked along with their family and friends. In the distance, leading the long procession, they could see Jesus, and clustering round him were all the other children of the village.

"Look at him," smiled Mary, "he's so tall and strong for twelve."

"And always in the middle of a crowd," laughed Joseph. "He's so full of fun he makes everyone happy."

The holiday flashed by far too quickly. Suddenly it was the last day and they were all packing up to go home again.

Mary and Joseph were far too busy to notice that Jesus was missing. He had gone to say goodbye to the temple, and, just for once, he had gone alone.

"I feel I really belong here, in my Father's house," sighed Jesus as he walked around the beautiful building. "I wish I could stay here forever, instead of learning to be a carpenter."

It was just then that he heard the angry voices. A great argument was going on in one of the temple courtyards. All the famous teachers in the land were quarreling with each other about God.

They were far too busy to notice a boy moving towards them. Yet he actually knew far more about God than they did.

"Who said that?" demanded the most important teacher of all as he spun around and saw Jesus for the first time. The country boy had asked them a question that was so hard none of them could answer it.

"Come here, boy," snapped the old man. "If you're so clever, you tell us the answer."

All day long those teachers fired difficult questions at Jesus, but he answered them all. "Whoever can he be?" they asked as their white beards wagged in amazement. "He's not like any other boy in the world."

By this time Mary and Joseph had set off for home. They thought Jesus must be walking with his friends or his aunts and uncles. So it was not until they camped for the night that they realized he was lost. "Something terrible must have happened," they gasped as they rushed back to Jerusalem.

Of course they should have looked for the Son of God in the temple, but they had kept the secret for so long they had almost forgotten who Jesus really was. Instead they dashed around the dark streets and noisy markets, searching desperately.

When at last they DID look in the temple, they saw a strange sight. A vast crowd had gathered round the old teachers, and in the very center stood Jesus. Everyone was listening to him in amazement.

"You shouldn't have worried about me," he said gently to Mary. "Now that I'm twelve I have to work for my real Father."

"Come home with us for a little longer," pleaded Mary. So Jesus went back to Nazareth and learned to be a fine carpenter.

No one in the village guessed his secret, but everybody loved him.

Matthew 3:1-12; Mark 1:1-8; |Luke 3:1-18; John 1:19-34

THE WILD MAN OF THE DESERT

SOMETHING VERY strange was happening in the desert. Usually no one went there, because it was nothing but sand, rocks and burning hot sun. Now suddenly great crowds of people were hurrying there to see a very odd looking man indeed.

"The time has come at last!" he shouted. "The King that God promised us has arrived!"

The man's hair was long and untidy and his clothes were dusty and rough, but the people strained to hear every word he said.

"Could he possibly be the Messiah himself?" whispered the people eagerly. But they were wrong. This strange man was old Elizabeth's son, John.

"Your job is to tell people who their real King is," his old mother had always told him. She had even let him into the great secret. His own cousin Jesus was actually the Messiah.

So John had spent years living alone out there in the desert, waiting for a message from God.

At last, one day it came. "John," said the voice of God, "when you see my Spirit floating down from heaven and resting on a man, you must tell my people he is their King."

"Get ready for God's new kingdom!" shouted John to the crowds who clustered round him. "Tell God you are sorry for the bad things you all do."

Near where he stood flowed the Jordan River. Stepping into the water, John said, "Come and let me baptize you to show your sins are washed away." Hundreds of people hurried into the river and John baptized them all.

One morning there was great excitement on the river bank. There seemed to be even more people waiting to be baptized than usual, but suddenly the crowds stepped back to make room for a group of very important looking men.

"We have been sent here by the priests in Jerusalem," they said to John, "to ask if you are the promised King." An excited silence settled over all the people. What would John say now?

"When your King does come," replied John at last, "I won't even be fit to undo his shoes."

"Who are you then?" they snapped crossly, but John was not even listening any more. He was standing in the water gazing up into the face of a man who stood above him on the bank. "This is the moment I've been waiting for all my life," he breathed.

"Will you baptize me too, cousin John?" smiled Jesus.

"What?" gasped John. "You ought to baptize me!"

"Please," persisted Jesus. "This is what God wants me to do."

As Jesus climbed out of the water a wonderful thing happened. The sky above his head seemed to open in a blaze of golden light and a beautiful dove fluttered down from heaven and rested on him. Then a great, echoing voice rumbled around the desert rocks. "This is my very own Son," said God. "I am wonderfully pleased with him."

"Here is your Messiah!" shouted John and the secret was out at last. The time had come for Jesus to show the world what God was really like.

THE BATTLE WITH SATAN

HE'S GOING IN the wrong direction!" exclaimed John as he watched his cousin Jesus walk away alone into the desert. "I've just told everyone who he is, so why doesn't he hurry to Jerusalem to be crowned King?"

But Jesus never did quite do what people expected him to.

He had been busy in the carpenter's shop for many years now. After Joseph died, he had helped Mary to look after his younger brothers and sisters and earned money for the family. Now he needed to be alone with God to talk about the new life that lay ahead of him.

For weeks he wandered about the rocky desert where there was nothing to eat, and every day he grew more hungry.

As he sat there alone, he thought about the plan he had made with his heavenly Father. They wanted people to live for ever, but they also knew that Jesus would have to die on a cross to make that possible. Jesus realized that would hurt him terribly, and how he wished there was some other way to save people from death.

"There he is," thought Satan, who had been watching Jesus all the time. "He's lonely, hungry and very sad. Now's my chance to make him do something wrong. That would spoil God's plans."

"If you REALLY are the Son of God," he said in a slimy voice, "then surely you've got enough power to turn these stones into bread. You don't have to sit there feeling hungry."

"I'm not going to use my power on myself," replied Jesus. "And my Father says there are more important things in life than eating."

Satan was cross, but he tried again. "No one's really going to believe you're God's Son," he said. "You must prove it. I'll take you to the temple in Jerusalem and you can jump off the roof. After all, God's promised that his angels will look after you."

"Yes," said Jesus, "but his rules say you must not make God angry by doing silly things like that."

Satan was beginning to feel worried. He had always found it so easy before to make people do what he wanted. "Look," he said, trying to sound nice, "I could make you King of the whole world NOW! All you would have to do is kneel and worship me."

Jesus was quiet for a long time. God would make him King of the world one day, but he would have to die on that cross first. Satan's way would be quicker and much less painful. God's enemy smiled nastily as he waited for Jesus to reply, but soon that smile turned into rage.

"Go away Satan!" shouted Jesus. "You know perfectly well it's against the rules to worship anyone but God."

As Satan stormed away furiously, Jesus fell to the ground too tired and hungry to stand up any longer. Then the many invisible angels who had been near him all the time suddenly appeared to comfort him.

"I feel better now," he smiled. "I am ready to go back and begin my Father's work."

THE WEDDING THAT NEARLY WENT WRONG

WHERE WILL you go now?" asked John when Jesus came back to the Jordan River, looking very dusty and thin.

"Home," smiled his cousin. "Some friends of our family are getting married soon. If I hurry I may be back in time for the wedding."

Jesus never seemed to go anywhere without making friends, and as he walked up the road all kinds of people went with him.

"If John's right, and this man is really the Son of God, we want to stay near him," they said to each other.

"Anyway," added a big fisherman called Peter, "just being with him makes me feel happy."

"Yes," sighed his brother Andrew, "it's a shame we have to go back to work."

"Why don't you all come with me to the wedding?" suggested Jesus, who seemed to know exactly what people were thinking.

The wedding had already begun when they all arrived. The bride and groom were delighted to see Jesus, because he always made parties more fun, and they welcomed his new friends.

But in the middle of all the laughter and happiness something went wrong. When one of the servants came and whispered to Mary, she turned very white and hurried into the kitchen.

"We've run out of wine," gasped the head waiter.

"Oh no!" exclaimed Mary. She knew the wedding would be completely spoiled now for the bride and groom and their families.

Everyone in all the villages around would laugh at them for being too poor to buy enough wine.

"Thank God my son Jesus is back," sighed Mary. "I'll go at once and ask him what we should do. He always seems to be able to help people out of trouble." Then she looked at all the servants and added, "Remember, whatever he tells you to do, you're to do it at once."

A few minutes later Jesus himself came into the kitchen. Pointing to the six large jars that stood in the corner he said, "Go to the well and fill them up with water."

"He must be mad," thought the head waiter. "We've run out of wine, not water!"

At the head of the table sat the most important man in the village, the guest of honor. When the servants heard him calling for more wine they were really worried. "What shall we do now?" they asked Jesus.

"Fill your jugs with the water from the jars and go and serve him," smiled Jesus.

"WITH WATER?" gasped the head waiter. "He'll be so cross we'll all be in trouble."

144

"Hurry up there," shouted the guest of honor, "I'm thirsty!"

The head waiter's hand was shaking so much it was hard to pour from the heavy jug. Then he shut his eyes tightly as he waited for the angry shout of disgust.

Instead the guest of honor smacked his lips and said, "Well done, bridegroom! This is the finest wine I have ever tasted."

Slowly the servant opened his eyes and looked right into the smiling face of Jesus.

THE DAY JESUS WAS ANGRY

JESUS STOOD GLARING around the temple, and his whole face was twisted with anger. "How dare you do this!" he shouted. His new friends gazed at him in amazement. He was usually so gentle and happy. Whatever could have upset him like this?

A few days after the wedding they had all set off to the great feast in Jerusalem. Jesus had hurried down the road, full of excitement, as he longed to be in the temple once again.

But when they arrived they had a dreadful shock. The beautiful, white, marble courtyards of God's house had been turned into a marketplace. Lambs and bulls were protesting loudly as they were penned up among the pillars. Birds in cages squawked angrily, and money clinked as men quarreled noisily, cheating each other over prices.

"My Father's house is supposed to be a place where people can pray in peace,"

thundered Jesus, "not a home for robbers. I'll have to put a stop to this."

"Oh no!" gasped his friends, who were already most alarmed. "It would be terribly dangerous for you to upset the priests. They're making a lot of money from this."

It was no good, Jesus would not listen. Picking up some ropes, he twisted them into a whip, and then into the middle of the market he charged.

"Get out of my Father's house!" he stormed as he sent the money tables crashing to the ground. Animals escaped and ran in all directions when Jesus knocked over their pens, and birds soared thankfully to freedom as their cages were opened wide.

Swish! crack! went the whip as startled people jumped for cover. Furious traders and delighted thieves crawled on the ground together, scrabbling for the golden coins. How they swore at the farmers who trampled on their fingers as they chased about after the bulls!

Peter, the fisherman, stood with his hands on his hips and laughed until he cried. "What a man!" he said admiringly as Jesus sent the last trader running out of the temple door.

The chief priests were also watching, and they were very angry. "One day, we will make that man extremely sorry for this," they growled.

As Jesus stood alone among the scattered remains of the market, all the anger suddenly died from his face. There, huddled nervously behind the marble pillars, crouched the people who had been too ill to run away. Throwing down his whip, Jesus hurried over and began to comfort them. His friends watched in amazement as lame people put down their crutches and began to dance; blind people shouted with delight as they looked at the temple for the first time; and little, white-faced children stopped coughing and started to laugh.

"This must really be the Son of God!" said Peter's young friend John. "I shall never forget this day as long as I live."

THE PRECIPICE

NAZARETH WAS buzzing with excitement. "We keep on hearing all kinds of stories about your son, Jesus," the village people said to Mary. "Is it true he can make people well?"

"Yes," smiled Mary. "Only the other day he healed a little boy, the son of one of the king's best friends."

"You must be proud of him," they all agreed.

One Sabbath morning, as they crowded into the little church they called the synagogue, they were delighted to see Jesus walking in through the door. "Look! He's going to preach the sermon," they whispered as they saw him opening the scroll.

"Today I want to read to you from the old book that Isaiah wrote," began Jesus, and as they listened the people were amazed. "Wherever did he learn to speak like this?" they muttered. "He sounds as if he really knows what he's talking about."

"But listen to what he's actually saying!" hissed someone, and the smiles of pride changed to frowns of anger as they sat up stiffly in their seats.

Jesus was reading words Isaiah had written hundreds of years before, all about God's Son, the Messiah.

"Today these words have come true," said Jesus. "I, your King, have come to make blind people see, to make sad people happy and to free Satan's prisoners."

There was a stunned silence in the little church.

"We've known this man since he was a boy," they muttered. "We can all remember his father Joseph, so he's telling lies when he says he's God's Son!"

The angry buzz turned into a roar of rage as people sprang to their feet and grabbed hold of Jesus roughly.

"Over the cliffs with this wicked liar!" yelled the people of Nazareth as they dragged Jesus out of the synagogue and up to the top of the hill.

"NO!" pleaded Mary. "He's telling the truth. He IS God's Son." But no one listened to her, and Satan smiled as he looked on.

Nearer and nearer the edge of the cliffs they dragged him.

"Over he'll go, head first, to his death!" laughed Satan. But the time had not yet come for Jesus to die, and right on the very edge of the precipice he turned and looked back into the faces of the people who had loved him all his life.

One by one their hands dropped and they stepped back ashamed and bewildered. How could they hurt someone who had always been so kind to them?

Slowly Jesus walked through the crowd and, putting his arm round Mary's shoulders, they walked away. "We can't live here now," said Jesus gently. "I'll take you to my friends, Peter and Andrew."

So the next day the whole family moved away from Nazareth and went to live in the fishing village of Capernaum by the seaside.

WHEN OLD GRANDMA DID NOT DIE

PETER WAS HAPPY as he sailed his boat home that day. It was good having Jesus living in their town now. "I've never liked sermons much," grinned the fisherman. "But I could listen to Jesus for hours."

"I hope he'll stay in Capernaum for ever," he said to his friends James and John as they pulled their boats up the beach.

Peter was whistling as he walked into his little cottage by the sea, but his happy mood disappeared very suddenly.

The fire was out and no food stood waiting for him. His wife looked as if she had been crying for hours when she told him the news. "It's our old Grandma," she sobbed. "She's terribly ill."

Next day, when Peter went to the synagogue, he had to fight his way through the great crowds who had come to hear Jesus preach.

"How's old Grandma today?" they all asked, because everyone in Capernaum loved the old lady.

"She's worse," replied Peter sadly. "We're afraid she's going to die."

Suddenly he felt a hand on his shoulder and, swinging around, he saw Jesus standing behind him. "Let me come and see her," he said kindly.

The old lady was lying on a mat in the corner of Peter's house, but she was so ill she did not even know Jesus was standing beside her.

Peter and his wife stood by anxiously as Jesus bent down and took the wrinkled old hands in his. "Come on, old Grandma," he said gently. "It's time to get better."

Suddenly the old lady's eyes flickered and slowly she sat up. "Fancy YOU coming to our little house," she said as she smiled at Jesus. "I must get up at once and cook you a special meal. Come on, daughter," she added as Jesus helped her to her feet, "light the fire quickly."

It was a wonderful dinner, for the old lady was a very good cook, and they were still eating when the evening shadows filled the room.

Suddenly a strange noise outside made old Grandma hurry to the window. "The street's full of people," she exclaimed. "It looks as if everyone in Capernaum has come to our house!"

"And they've brought all the sick folk with them," added her daughter in amazement.

As Jesus hurried out of the house, voices called to him from all directions:

"Please, make my baby better."

"Heal my poor husband's leg, so he can work again."

"You made old Grandma well again, so I've brought you my grandad; he's blind."

It took Jesus many hours to touch and heal each person in that crowd, but he did.

When the last person walked home, happy and well, Peter was already snoring loudly, but early next morning, when he woke up, Jesus was gone. "We must find him!" said Peter to the other fishermen. "We can't let him leave Capernaum now."

"I have to go on to other towns," explained Jesus when at last they caught up with him on the dusty road. "I must tell people everywhere how much God loves them."

Sadly they walked back to their boats. Life was going to be very dull now without Jesus.

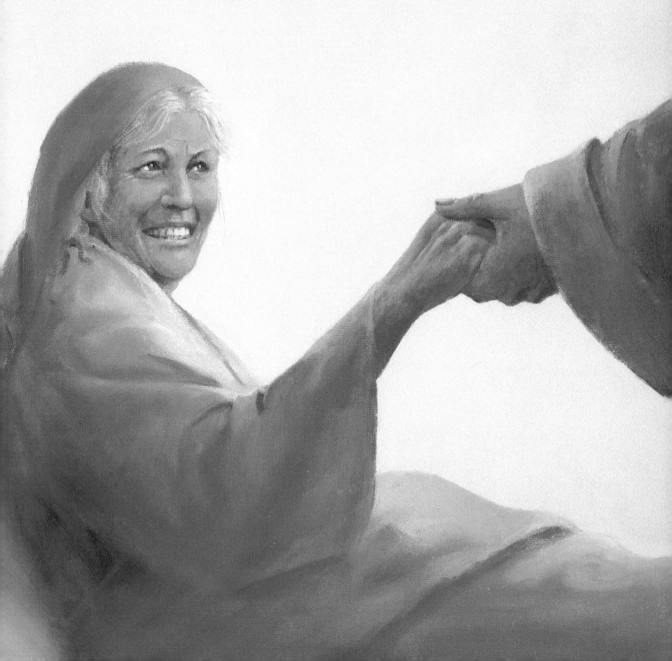

A SURPRISE FOR PETER

THERE'LL BE NO dinner for the children again today," sighed Peter as he and his brother rowed ashore one morning. How was he going to tell his wife and old Grandma that once again they had worked all night without catching a single fish?

"Whatever's happening on the beach?" said Andrew. "Who are all those people?"

"Jesus is back!" exclaimed their friends James and John. "And it looks as if hundreds of people have come to hear him."

Peter felt really cross. He longed to rush up to his new friend and tell him all his worries, but Jesus was hidden in the middle of a great crowd of strangers. "They won't be able to hear a word he says," growled Peter, "if they all keep pushing each other like that." He had been fishing all night, and he was tired. But just as he was walking miserably home to bed he heard Jesus call his name. "Peter, will you row me out a little way in your boat?"

For hours they rocked in the sunshine with Jesus sitting where everyone on the beach could see and hear him perfectly. Some of the stories he told were so funny people ached with laughter, while others made even the grown-ups cry.

"Thank you Peter," smiled Jesus at last. "Now let's go fishing."

"What!" exclaimed Peter. "At noon?" and he burst out laughing. This man might know a lot about carpentry, but he certainly knew nothing about fishing.

"Please," persisted Jesus.

"But you can't catch fish in this lake when the sun's shining," grinned the fishermen. "And anyway, there just aren't any fish about these days."

Still Jesus sat there, smiling, until in the end Peter and his brother had to throw the nets over the side of the boat.

Almost at once an extraordinary thing happened. They caught such a huge school of fish the boat nearly capsized!

"Come out here and help us!" yelled Peter waving frantically to James and John.

The nets were almost breaking as the four fishermen dragged them out of the water, and soon both the boats were so full of silvery fish they almost sank.

"I never saw such a catch in my life," cried Peter, flinging himself down in front of Jesus. "You shouldn't come near a man like me. I'm always breaking God's rules."

"But God wants people to know how much he longs to forgive them," said Jesus. "Will you leave your fishing and help me to tell them all about God?"

Peter was so pleased he hardly knew what to say.

"I need to find twelve men who will be my special helpers," said Jesus as he looked at Andrew, James and John. "Will you come with me as well?"

"But we're only fishermen," they gasped.

"I need all kinds of different people," smiled Jesus, "Now you go to market and sell those fish. You will make enough money to look after your families while you are away."

THE HOLE IN
THE ROOF

THE PEOPLE OF Capernaum were amazed next day, when into their little town rode some of the most important men in the land. They were called Pharisees, and they were very proud of themselves because they always kept God's rules. But they had quite forgotten to love people.

Hearing so many stories about Jesus, they wanted to come and see what was happening.

"Jesus is in Peter's house," they were told. "But there's a huge crowd in there already." The famous teachers elbowed their way rudely into the fisherman's hut and sent old Grandma scuttling off to fetch them some wine.

Jesus did not even seem to notice them; he was too busy talking to the thin, ragged people who had walked miles to hear him. "You are poor, hungry and sad now," he told them, "and no one seems to care about you, so I have come to tell you how much God loves you and that he is planning many lovely things for you in heaven."

"Why does he waste his time on beggars when he could be talking to people like us?" sniffed the Pharisees.

By this time so many people were squashed close to Jesus that there was no more room in the house and latecomers had to stand outside. Yet they were all listening so intently that a strange noise on the roof made them jump.

Dust and plaster began to fall from the ceiling, showering the important visitors, while old Grandma hopped about in agitation.

"This is outrageous!" stormed the Pharisees as they saw a large hole appearing above their heads. Down swung a mattress, lowered by four ropes, and on it lay a man who had not been able to move for many years. His friends could not reach Jesus through the crowd so they had climbed the outside staircase and ripped open the flat roof.

Jesus knew exactly what was troubling the man. Night and day he lay worrying about the bad things he had done long ago when he could still walk.

"You are forgiven," said Jesus gently.

"Only God can forgive sin!" thundered the Pharisees jumping to their feet. "How dare you say you are God!"

"I will prove who I am," replied Jesus, and looking down at the man he said, "Get up, and carry your own bed home."

The people gasped in wonder as they saw him scramble to his feet, but the Pharisees pushed their way angrily outside. "Jesus must be stopped!" they said in disgust.

But by evening, they were even more angry!

Jesus had asked one of the worst and most hated men in Capernaum to be his disciple, too. Matthew was so thrilled, he invited Jesus to his house so he could meet all the other bad people in the town.

The Pharisees were horrified when they looked in through the windows. "Why is Jesus eating and making friends with people that THAT?" they called out to Peter. "We wouldn't dream of even speaking to bad men ourselves!"

"He's helping them to change," laughed Peter. As he hurried back to the party the Pharisees climbed onto their camels and rode angrily home.

155

JESUS WAS NOT TOO LATE

JAIRUS SAT BY his daughter's bed and held her hot, sticky hand. Every day she had been getting worse. "If only Jesus was still in Capernaum," he thought miserably. "It's weeks since he went off to other towns and now my little girl is dying." Jairus was a very rich and important man, but he would have given all the money he had to see his little girl well again.

Outside in the street he suddenly heard cries of excitement and running footsteps.

"Jesus is back!" someone shouted. "He's just landed on the beach in Peter's boat."

Jairus sprang up and rushed out of the house. Jesus might just be in time after all. But he must be quick.

Everyone seemed to be running in the same direction and they all got in his way. Poor Jairus felt he was trapped in a bad dream. When he finally arrived on the shore he was so out of breath he could hardly speak. He just flung himself down before Jesus and bowed his head.

"No Jew ever bows to anyone but God," gasped the people in amazement. "He should know that, he's in charge of our synagogue. Whatever will his friends the Pharisees say?"

"Please!" gasped Jairus. "My daughter is dying."

"I'll come at once," replied Jesus, helping him to his feet.

"We must hurry!" sobbed Jairus, but the narrow streets were packed with people waiting for Jesus. They pushed around him so tightly he could hardly breathe and no one would let them through.

When Jesus stopped to heal a poor woman who had been ill for twelve years, Jairus could stand it no longer. "If you don't get there soon," he exclaimed, "you'll be too late!"

He was nearly frantic when he caught

sight of his servant pushing through the crowd and when he saw the man's face he knew what he had come to say. "Your little girl has just died," he whispered. "You don't need to bother the teacher any more."

"Don't worry, Jairus," said Jesus quickly. "Just trust me." He did not only love the poor and the bad. He cared about wealthy people just as much.

As they walked towards the house they heard a terrible sound. All the neighbors were crying loudly and playing dismal music on their flutes. "Even Jesus can't help now she's dead," they wailed.

"I have come to wake her up," said Jesus, and how they sneered at him because they knew that was impossible.

The rest of the family and all their friends filled the house and they glared angrily at Jesus for coming too late.

On into the dark, little bedroom he walked and shut them all outside. Only Peter, James, John and the little girl's parents were allowed to see what was going to happen.

"Little one, it's time to wake up," said Jesus, using the words Mary had spoken to him every morning when he was a child.

Life surged back into her still body, and her white cheeks turned a rosy pink.

"Give her some breakfast," smiled Jesus. Soon the little girl was surrounded by happy faces and quietly Jesus and the fishermen left the house.

NEVER TOO BUSY FOR CHILDREN

WHEN JESUS IS crowned King and lives in a palace," said James as they all trudged along the hot, dusty road, "I hope he'll make me prime minister."

"But I'm more important than you are," said Peter quickly.

"No, you're only a fisherman," argued Matthew. "Jesus would need someone clever, like me."

The disciples' voices were beginning to sound angry, and Peter looked over his shoulder at Jesus.

"Look!" he said anxiously. "The Lord is so exhausted he can hardly walk. Everyday it's the same, crowds of people around him all the time, and always moving on. He often has no time to eat or sleep. When we get to the next town, I'm going to get rid of everyone and let him have a long rest in the shade."

Down in the valley a group of children was jumping about with excitement as they watched the road. For weeks they had been waiting for Jesus to visit their town. Now the great day had come at last, and their mothers had scrubbed them clean and dressed them in their best.

"Perhaps he'll mend my twisted leg," said a little boy with a crutch.

"He might even touch my eyes and make me see," added Hannah, who had been born blind.

"I want to hear his wonderful stories," put in an older boy. "I wish he'd hurry up."

Into the town surged the crowds who always followed Jesus, and the children felt suddenly shy.

"Come on," laughed their mothers, and pushed them towards Jesus, who was sitting by the village well.

But a very big man was standing right in front of him, glaring at them. "Off you go!" shouted Peter. "Jesus is far too tired to be bothered by noisy children."

"But they've waited so long," protested the mothers, "and he may never come here again." The smiles died from the children's faces and the little blind girl began to cry.

"Go on!" roared Peter. "Before I take my stick to you!"

"Oh dear," they sighed as sadly they turned away. "We should have known Jesus is much too important to bother about children.

"How COULD you send them away!" said a very different voice. "Let them come to me at once."

They could hardly believe it was true when they looked back to see Jesus holding out his arms. "I'm never too busy for children," he smiled. "Come and let me see those eyes of yours, Hannah, and where's that bad leg of yours, Mark?"

"How do you know our names?" they gasped.

"I knew you all before you were babies," laughed Jesus as a little, fat girl climbed onto his knee.

For hours they clustered closely round him, all talking at once. Somehow he managed to hear everyone and made them all feel safer and happier than they had ever done before.

"You'd think he'd never been tired in his life," muttered Peter.

"Remember this," said Jesus, looking up at his disciples over the heads of the children. "No one can get into my kingdom if they are proud. You have to become like one of these children." And he smiled down into the sparkling eyes of the girl who had once been blind.

THE VACATION THAT WENT WRONG

ONE DAY SOME men brought Jesus terrible news. "King Herod has killed your cousin John." For months poor John had been shut in a dungeon because he had told the king and queen just how bad they were. Now they had cut off his head.

Jesus felt so sad he longed to be alone for a while. "We all need a vacation," he said to his disciples. "You look tired. Let's row over to the other side of the lake and find a really lonely place to camp."

As the boat skimmed over the water, leaving the crowds far behind, they all began to feel better. "No more people pushing around us," laughed Peter as the boat crunched on a sandy shore. "This place is just right for a vacation. Nothing but grass and birds."

They hardly had time to build their camp fire before they were groaning in dismay. Surging towards them along the beach came the crowds. They must have seen Jesus slip away, and thousands of them had dashed round the lakeside to catch up with him.

One of the first to arrive was a little boy. He had been walking for hours because he was so desperate to see Jesus. He hadn't even had time to eat the food his mother had packed for his journey.

"Oh NO!" grumbled Peter. "Send them away, Lord."

But Jesus could see how sad and worried most of those people were. They had come to him because no one else would help; he couldn't just turn them away. Soon he was talking to everyone, cheering them all up and healing the sick.

By evening the little boy was still clutching his picnic basket, but the stories Jesus had told were so exciting he had still forgotten to eat. As he opened the lid, the bread and fish smelled good, but he couldn't help wondering if Jesus had anything for his supper.

"He looks so tired and hungry," thought the boy, and closing the lid again he crept towards the disciples.

"Come on, Master," they were saying crossly. "Send the people away so we can have our vacation."

"But they're hungry," said Jesus. "They rushed here so quickly, most of them forgot to bring any food. It's a long walk to the shops and the children are tired. We must give them something before they go."

"Two hundred silver pieces wouldn't feed them all!" protested Philip, who knew they had no money left.

"There's a boy here," said Andrew. "He says he wants you to have his picnic, Lord. Look! Five rolls and two fish. At least YOU won't be hungry."

Jesus bent down and took the basket from the boy, who never, ever forgot the way Jesus smiled as he said, "Thank you."

"Tell everyone to sit down on the grass," said Jesus and, after he had thanked God, he opened the basket and began producing fish, tucked inside the bread rolls.

"One, two ... ten, eleven ... twenty, thirty!" counted the boy. "Whatever's happening? Jesus is bringing enough food out of my basket to feed everyone! Yet I only had enough for myself!"

As the happy, well fed crowds walked home under the stars that night, the little boy knew that all he ever wanted to do was to follow Jesus.

A STORM AT SEA

THE LITTLE BOAT in the middle of the lake almost capsized as the great waves crashed against it and the wind and rain beat the faces of the frightened disciples.

"I knew this storm was coming!" shouted Peter, but his voice was lost in a crack of thunder. He remembered how he had tried to warn them earlier as they stood on the beach. But Jesus had said, "We must escape from here at once. You row back to Capernaum and I'll go up to the hills."

Everything had gone wrong after the huge picnic on the beach. The people were so excited they wanted to march straight to Jerusalem and crown Jesus as King. "He'll stop the Romans telling us what to do and taking our money," they had shouted. "There are thousands of us here now, let's leave at once."

But Jesus had not come to be an earthly King in a palace. When he tried to explain that, the people would not listen. "Grab him," they shouted. "He MUST be our King." That is why Jesus had to disappear; but when they found he was gone, the people were furious.

Back in the boat, Peter was wishing that Jesus had come with them. "We're going to sink in a minute," he thought as his boat began to fill with water.

"Whatever's that?" gasped Andrew as another flash of lightning broke the darkness. Over the heaving waves a frightening shape was moving slowly towards them. "It's a ghost!" they shrieked, and dropping their oars they dived for the bottom of the boat. Only Peter was left peering into the storm.

"Don't be frightened, it's only me."

Through the screaming wind came the voice they loved so much, and suddenly Peter knew the only thing he wanted was to be close to Jesus again. He didn't stop to think what he was doing, he just jumped out of the boat and ran towards Jesus over the waves. "Everything will be alright when I reach him," he thought. But suddenly he realized what he was doing! "People can't walk on water," he thought. "I'll drown."

As soon as he stopped looking at Jesus, Peter saw how big the waves were and began to sink. "Lord, save me!" he screamed.

In a flash Jesus was there and, bending down, he took Peter's hand. "You stopped trusting me," he said gently.

Soon they were safely back in the boat and instantly the wind and rain died away and the waves turned into ripples.

It was good to be back in Capernaum, but old Grandma hardly had time to cook their breakfast before the crowds had caught up with them again.

"We want another free dinner!" they demanded. But when they found they couldn't make Jesus do exactly what they wanted, giving them easy, comfortable lives, many of them began to hate him.

At sunset Jesus stood looking sadly at the stream of people walking away from Capernaum. "We're going home," lots of them were saying. "Jesus is crazy! We're not listening to him anymore."

"Will you leave me too?" asked Jesus looking at his disciples.

"Where could we go," smiled Peter. "You're the only one who knows the way to heaven."

THE BOY WHO RAN AWAY

JERUSALEM WAS FULL of whispers. When Jesus arrived for the feast that year, everyone seemed to be staring at him. "He's a good man," said some people.

"No!" others replied. "He says he's God, so he must be a liar."

"Just look at him now!" exclaimed the Pharisees in horror when they saw Jesus sitting in a back street surrounded by most of the city's robbers, murderers and bad women.

"If he was really God, he certainly wouldn't go near people like that," they sniffed. But when they heard what Jesus was saying they were even more angry:

"There was once a farmer who had two sons.

" 'I wish I lived in the city,' the younger boy was always thinking. 'I'd go to parties every night and eat and drink till morning. I'm sick of this boring farm.'

"In the end he asked his father for his share of the family money, and off he went.

"A big house and smart clothes soon bought him lots of friends, but they only liked him because he gave them presents and asked them to his parties.

"One terrible day he realized his money was all gone. 'Never mind,' he thought. 'My friends will look after me.' But they didn't want to know him any more, now he was poor. No one in the whole city would give him a job, so in the end he wandered out into the country.

" 'You can look after my pigs,' said a farmer, but he was so mean he gave the boy nothing to eat.

"The pigs smelled dreadful, and the rotting rubbish they ate was even worse, but he was so hungry he scooped it up from the muddy ground and began to eat. 'Why did I ever leave my father?' he sobbed. 'HE would never treat his servants like this. They're all well fed and warmly dressed.'

"Suddenly, he jumped to his feet. 'That's what I'll do,' he exclaimed. 'I'll go home and tell my father how sorry I am. Perhaps he'll let me work as his servant.' "

All those people in that back street knew just how the boy in the story must have felt. "Would the father turn his son away?" they wondered as they listened eagerly.

"When the boy was still a long way from home his father saw him, because he had been watching for his son all the time he was away. He ran down the road with his arms open wide, and the thin ragged boy stumbled towards him.

" 'Father, I'm sorry,' he cried, as his father kissed him.

" 'Come on,' smiled the father. 'Let's get you into some clean clothes. Tonight we'll have a feast to welcome you back.' Putting his arm round the boy, they walked home together."

A great sigh of relief went around the crowd. Surely Jesus was telling them that God would forgive them too, however bad they were, if only they would ask him.

DANGER ON THE LONELY ROAD

"GO AND ARREST this Jesus," the Pharisees told the temple police. "We can't have everyone in Jerusalem thinking he's the Messiah!"

But those policemen made a big mistake. They stopped and listened to what Jesus was saying.

"Love people who hate you."

"Did you hear that?" they gasped.

"Be kind to people who do mean things to you."

The policemen stood with their mouths open.

"God's rules say we must love God and other people as much as we love ourselves," said one of the Pharisees, trying to trick Jesus with a difficult question. "But surely a good Jew can only love good people?"

"I'll tell you a story that will answer that," said Jesus, as everyone gathered eagerly round him. "Once a man was traveling alone between Jerusalem and Jericho."

"Agh!" gasped the crowd. They all knew what a lonely, dangerous road that was. It wound between towering rocks, where robbers lurked in the dark shadows waiting to pounce. Everyone hated to be alone on that road.

"Suddenly," continued Jesus, "out jumped a gang of ragged men armed with sticks and knives. They stole his money, beat him cruelly and ran away leaving him bleeding on the ground.

"Not long afterwards a priest walked by on his way to the temple in Jerusalem. 'Tut, tut,' he said when he saw the man lying there covered in blood and flies. 'Poor man. But if I stop to help, I'll spoil my temple clothes.' So he hurried on past.

"Hour after hour, the injured man lay longing for someone to come. At last he heard footsteps, and around the corner came a Pharisee. 'He spends his life telling people about God's rules,' he thought. 'Surely he'll help.'

"Nervously the teacher crept over and peered down at the wounded man. 'Suppose the robbers who attacked this man are still hiding here,' he shivered. 'They'll probably hurt me too and steal my money.' He soon disappeared in the distance.

" 'No one will come now,' thought the poor man. 'It's beginning to get dark and by morning I'll be dead.'

"It was then that he heard the 'clop, clop' of a donkey's hooves, but his heart sank when he opened his eyes. It was only a Samaritan. He CERTAINLY wouldn't help. (The Samaritans and the Jews were such enemies they wouldn't even speak to each other.)

"How astonished he was when he felt kind hands lifting his head. Someone was giving him a drink and rubbing soothing ointment into his painful cuts. Strong arms lifted him onto a donkey and took him all the way to a hotel.

" 'Why is this Samaritan being so kind?' he wondered when he found himself lying in a clean, comfortable bed. 'They stole all my money,' he managed to say.

" 'Don't worry,' smiled the Samaritan. 'You can stay here until you're better; I'm paying the bill for you.' "

"Which man in that story really LOVED the injured man?" asked Jesus. "Was it the good Jew who always kept the rules?"

"No," said the teacher uncomfortably. "It was the Samaritan."

"Then you go and love people like that too," said Jesus.

"Well, where is he?" demanded the Pharisees when the policemen came back without Jesus. Looking very embarrassed they replied, "We never heard anyone talking like this before."

FEAR ON THE MOUNTAIN

THEY ONLY JUST escaped from Jerusalem in time. By the last day of the feast the Pharisees were so furious with Jesus, they were throwing stones at him.

Whenever Jesus was sad or worried he always went off alone to talk to God. On the way back from Jerusalem he disappeared for so long that his disciples set out to look for him. "Who do YOU think I am?" Jesus asked when they found him.

"You're the Messiah that all those prophets told us about," smiled Peter.

"You're right, Peter!" replied Jesus. "But don't forget what the prophets said would happen to the Messiah. Soon I'll have to go back to Jerusalem again. This time the priests and Pharisees will beat me and kill me and I will be dead for three days."

"NO!" shouted Peter indignantly. "You have so much power, you could easily stop them."

"Be quiet, Peter!" said Jesus firmly. "You sound like Satan. He would love to spoil God's plans." Turning to the others he added, "Remember this! Following me will always be difficult. But I shall be watching the things you do for me secretly, and one day I will reward you in front of everyone."

Peter, James and John were the three disciples who loved Jesus the most. They couldn't bear to think of him being hurt, so for a week they hardly spoke.

"Come on, you three," said Jesus at last, "let's climb that mountain, it might cheer you up."

Just as they puffed up the last steep bit of the path, the three fishermen saw a very strange sight. Jesus began to shine as if there was a powerful light inside him, and his dusty old clothes shimmered and sparkled like frosty snow in bright sunlight.

"Who's that talking to him?" gasped Peter as he clutched the others in terror.

"It's Moses and Elijah," they answered breathlessly. "They must have come down from heaven."

"Hush," whispered Peter. "Listen to what they're all saying." But they soon wished they HADN'T listened.

"He's telling them too," muttered Peter, "about God's plan for him to die in Jerusalem. Surely it can't be right!"

Peter was always doing things without thinking first, so he burst into the conversation. "Let us build you three little tents," he shouted. "Then you can all stay here for ever."

Suddenly they were wrapped in a shining cloud which covered them completely. "This is my own much loved Son," said the thundering voice of God. "You must listen to him."

After that they were so frozen with fear, even Peter could think of nothing to say. They just lay flat on the ground and covered their heads.

When someone touched them they cowered away like frightened animals, but looking up they saw Jesus, standing there alone. He was just as dusty and tattered as usual, as he smiled kindly down on them. "Don't be frightened," he said gently. "Come on, there's work for us to do down there in the valley."

THE MAN WHO SAID NO TO JESUS

I WISH I WAS RICH enough to live in a house like that!" exclaimed Judas Iscariot, one of the disciples of Jesus. They were coming home to Capernaum after weeks on the dusty roads. Peter was longing for his boat and the smell of the sea, but Judas had always loved money.

"The man who owns that house is the richest man in town," smiled Andrew. "But it's odd how miserable he always looks."

Just then the door of the grand house flew open and the rich man himself rushed out into the street. "Good sir!" he called to Jesus. "Tell me how to live for ever. I've kept God's rules all my life, but I'm still not sure if he's pleased with me."

Jesus looked at the ragged beggars huddled miserably in the gutters. Old people who had never had enough to eat and babies crying desperately for the food their mothers could not give to them.

Then he looked down into the rich man's eager face, and very gently he said, "I want you to be my disciple. Will you sell all you have and use the money to feed poor people like these?"

The rich man looked around at his fine house, the beautiful furniture and the fast horses in the stable. Slowly the excited smile faded from his face and, turning away, he walked back into his grand house. The great front door closed quietly behind him.

For a long time Jesus stood in the street gazing sadly after him. He loved that young man so much. "How hard it is for the rich to come into my kingdom," he sighed. "It's like a camel, loaded high with luggage, trying to squeeze through a tiny gate in the city wall. The one they call the Needle's Eye. Everything he is carrying has to be unloaded first."

"Can't rich men follow you then?" demanded Judas Iscariot.

"With God's help everything is possible," replied Jesus, and with one last sad look at the rich man's house he went off down the street.

"Now you're home, you and Jesus can pay your tax!" Peter jumped. He had dashed straight down to the lakeside to see if his boat was all right, and run straight into the tax man!

"But we haven't any money!" protested Peter, feeling in his empty purse.

"By this time tomorrow, you WILL pay," threatened the man, and Peter hurried home in great alarm.

"What shall we do, Lord?" he said when he found Jesus sitting by old Grandma's fire.

"Take your fishing line down to the lake, Peter," replied Jesus. "Inside the mouth of the first fish you catch, you will find a silver coin. Give that to the tax man for both of us."

"There you are!" said Peter triumphantly to the tax man next day. "There's NOTHING my Master can't do!"

THE MAN WHO SAID THANK YOU

IT WAS EVENING, and the wind moaned around the lonely hillside. In the distance the lights of the village twinkled cosily, but the ten men who crouched in the shadows knew they could never go home again. They had leprosy and gradually their bodies were rotting away. Everyone else was so afraid of catching the illness they had driven them out of the village to live alone among the rocks.

Suddenly, all ten men jumped to their feet. Shadows were moving towards them from the village. Every night their wives and daughters brought them food and water, but they laid their baskets on the ground a long way from the men.

"If only I was allowed to touch my daughter," thought one of the lepers miserably. He felt even more lonely than the other nine, because he was a Samaritan. He knew the rest hated him for that.

Something strange was happening that evening. Instead of hurrying home the women were waving their arms and shouting. "Listen!" they called. "We've got some wonderful news! A man called Jesus is going around healing people. EVEN LEPERS!"

The ten men could hardly eat their food that night, they were so excited.

"Suppose he really could make us well?" one of them asked.

"But our village is so small and quiet. Important people like him would never bother to come here," said another.

"We should keep watching the road, just in case," they all agreed. "It would be terrible to miss him if he DID come."

"Even if he came here," thought the Samaritan sadly to himself, "He wouldn't want to heal me."

Everyday they crouched as near to the road as they dared. They hardly noticed the burning sun, the flies or the dust; Jesus was their only hope.

"Come on," said Jesus to his disciples one day, "we're going to Jerusalem."

"Lord!" they gasped. "You know the priests and Pharisees are plotting to kill you."

Jesus looked at them sadly. He had explained so many times that it was part of God's plan for him to die and then rise again, but still they would not believe it.

"Why are we taking this road?" grumbled Peter. "It's miles out of our way." Jesus only smiled. He knew all about those ten lepers and how long they had waited.

"He's coming at last!" they exclaimed when they saw a huge crowd appearing in the distance. "Jesus, have mercy on us!" they yelled as loudly as they could. "Suppose he takes no notice, because we're lepers," they thought desperately.

But of course Jesus stopped right in the middle of the road. "Go to the priest," he shouted back, "and when he sees you are well, he will let you go home to your families."

Wild with excitement they all turned and dashed away, and as they ran their bodies were made perfectly well again. Only the Samaritan stopped and looked down at himself in wonder. "He's healed ME too!" he yelled in a loud voice, as he began to run back. "Thank you," he shouted as he knelt before Jesus in the road.

"Weren't there ten of you?" said Jesus sadly. "Are you the only one who bothers to say thank you?"

Luke 19:1-10

THE MAN WHO WAS NOT TALL ENOUGH

NOBODY IN JERICHO liked Zacchaeus. "He's a greedy little liar," they all said. "Fancy working for the Romans! He tells us they want even more of our money than they really do, so he can keep back some for himself. He's made himself rich with OUR money!"

People never spoke to him in the street, and every night he sat alone in his grand house eating food fit for a party, but no one ever came to share it. Zacchaeus pretended he did not care, but inside he was desperately lonely.

One day, as he worked in his office he heard a great buzz of excitement outside in the street. "He's coming past on his way up to Jerusalem," everyone was saying.

"Who's coming?" Zacchaeus asked one of his servants.

"Jesus of Nazareth," he told him.

Zacchaeus began to tremble. For three years now he had been hearing stories about this man. The piles of gold coins on his desk suddenly seemed unimportant. He knew he just wanted to see Jesus.

His servants were astounded when he jumped up and dashed out into the street. "I'll have to get to the front of this crowd," he thought. "I'm so short I can't see over their heads."

"Go away, Zacchaeus," everyone said as he tried to squeeze past them, and they prodded him back with their elbows. "We don't want Jesus to see you; you're a disgrace to the town."

"I'll run on ahead," he thought desperately, "and climb that old sycamore tree I used to play in when I was a boy. If I hide among the leaves, I can look down and see everything, but no one will see me."

174

The sight of a fat, little man struggling up a tree would have made everyone laugh, but no one saw Zacchaeus; they were too busy watching for Jesus.

It was easy to guess which man was Jesus and, as he clung nervously to the branches, Zacchaeus thought he had never seen anyone with such a kind face before. It made him remember all the bad things he had done and he longed to start all over again.

The next minute he nearly fell out of the tree with surprise. Jesus stopped and looked straight up at him through the leaves. "Zacchaeus, come down. I'm on my way to stay with you."

"He knows who I am, and he STILL wants to come to my house!" gasped Zacchaeus.

The good people of Jericho were jealous. "WE'RE the kind of people Jesus should visit," they sniffed, "not nasty men like that."

"It was for bad people that I came," said Jesus, "so that I could help them to change."

What a party they had. Zacchaeus could not remember ever being so happy. "I am going to give half my money to the poor," he told everyone. "And after that I will pay back four times as much to everyone whom I have cheated."

"Today," smiled Jesus, "God has saved you."

175

THE MAN WHO LIVED IN THE DARK

BARTIMAEUS HAD lived in the dark all his life. "Spare a coin for a poor, blind man," he would cry as he groped his way round Jericho.

"Get out of the way, you dirty, old beggar," shouted angry voices. No one ever cared that he was hungry. Even the donkeys stepped on him as he huddled by the roadside.

The only day when he felt safe was the Sabbath. The town was quiet then and the shops were shut. He used to feel his way to the synagogue, but he never dared to go

inside. People didn't like sitting next to smelly beggars while they worshiped God.

He stood outside and listened, because he wanted to hear the rabbi reading about the great King who was coming one day. "He will make the blind see." Those words gave Bartimaeus enough hope to go on living.

"Whatever is happening?" wondered Bartimaeus one day. Jericho seemed even busier than usual. The darkness that surrounded him was full of hurrying footsteps and excited voices.

"You're cluttering up the road," someone shouted. "Don't you know Jesus is in Jericho?"

"Who's he?" asked Bartimaeus bitterly.

"Stupid beggar!" they replied. "He's the great King that God promised us. He's on his way up to Jerusalem to be crowned."

"Where is he?" gasped Bartimaeus, but no one bothered to answer him.

"This is my chance!" he thought as he blundered through the crowded streets, bumping into people and colliding with camels. "Help me to find Jesus!" he kept on calling, but no one would listen.

"I'll wait for him by the city gate," he decided at last. "He's bound to pass that way."

It sounded so easy, but Jesus came by with such a huge crowd, poor Bartimaeus found himself pushed over in the mud. "Jesus, help me!" he shouted as loudly as he could, but people stepped on him as he tried to struggle to his feet.

"Be quiet!" they told him. "Jesus is going to be the greatest King in the world. He's too busy for beggars."

"But the rabbi said God's King would make the blind see," protested Bartimaeus and, taking a deep breath, he tried just one more time. "Jesus, HELP ME!"

The noises all around Jesus were deafening, but suddenly he stopped. "Bring that blind man here," he told Peter.

The big fisherman had to fight his way through the people, but at last he found Bartimaeus lying like a heap of rags on the ground. "Cheer up!" he said as he helped him to his feet. "Jesus is calling for you."

No one had ever touched the beggar with kind hands before. Was he dreaming?

"What do you want me to do for you?" said the gentlest voice he had ever heard.

"Lord, I want to see," stammered the blind man and, as he opened his eyes, the very first thing he saw was the face of Jesus.

"Let me come with you," he pleaded. "I can't stay here alone in Jericho."

"Come on then," smiled Jesus, and as the other disciples gathered around him, Bartimaeus knew he would never feel lonely again.

THE DAY JESUS CRIED

EVERYONE WAS going wild with excitement, cheering and jumping up and down. "Jesus is on his way; he's coming to the feast!"

As soon as the people of Jerusalem heard the news, they dashed out of the city and up the road to meet him. "Look, he's riding a young donkey!" they exclaimed. "The prophets said our Messiah would come to us like that! Our King is here at last!" They had no flags, so they pulled palm leaves from the trees and waved them instead.

The disciples were just as excited as everyone else. They had quite forgotten that Jesus had told them he was going to die in Jerusalem. "When he's King, we'll help him to rule the land," they thought happily, "and everyone will think how important we are."

"And I'll look after all his money," thought Judas Iscariot with a cunning smile. "Soon I shall be very rich."

"Kings ride over carpets," someone yelled, so they all pulled off their coats and laid them down in the road.

"Make way for the great King!" The shouting echoed around the hills, but as Jesus looked down on Jerusalem, spread out like a map below him, he felt so sad that he cried. He knew that in just a few years' time the Romans would kill thousands of Jews and drive them away from their land.

As he looked at all the happy faces around him he also knew that in less than a week their excitement would have changed to anger. These smiling people would soon be shouting for him to be killed. "Oh, Jerusalem, Jerusalem," he sighed. "Today your God has come to save you. I wanted to keep you

178

safe like a mother hen looks after her chicks, but you won't let me."

When the great procession finally arrived in Jerusalem, the city was in an uproar. "Have you all gone mad?" raged the chief priests and Pharisees. "Jesus! Tell the people to be quiet at once."

"If the people didn't shout, the very stones of Jerusalem would cry out in praise of me," replied Jesus softly.

"What are we going to DO?" thundered Caiaphas the High Priest behind the locked doors of his house. "The whole world seems to follow this man. We must kill him at once."

"How can we arrest him?" the others argued. "The people wouldn't let us."

"Then we must turn the people against him," whispered one of the Pharisees.

"And find out where he goes to at night," added another. "Perhaps if we offered enough money, one of his disciples would show us; then we could pounce on him."

Smiling nastily and rubbing their hands together, they slipped away into the shadows.

THE TRAITOR

THE STREETS OF Jerusalem were dark and quiet but, inside all the houses, families were gathering together for the Passover feast. It was a very special celebration meal when everyone ate roast lamb.

"This is the night when we remember how God rescued us from being slaves in Egypt," parents would tell the children.

"And the lambs died instead of us," the oldest boy in every family would reply.

In a little upstairs room, the disciples were also preparing their special meal, but everything seemed to be going wrong for them. They were quarreling again!

"I'm not doing that; it's a servant's job," snapped Matthew.

"And I'm far too important to wash feet!" bellowed Peter. Because the streets were so dusty, someone always had to wash away the dirt before people went indoors, but no one wanted that job. Jesus looked sadly at the angry faces of his friends; then quietly he knelt down and began to wash their feet himself.

"You mustn't do that, Lord!" the disciples exclaimed in horror.

"I'm doing it because I love you," replied Jesus, "but you must learn to love and serve each another."

Feeling very ashamed of themselves they all sat down to their supper, but Jesus seemed too sad to eat. "One of you is planning to betray me," he sighed.

"None of us would ever do such a thing!" they all protested, but Jesus was looking straight at Judas Iscariot.

The little, fat man loved money, and all the week Satan had been whispering in his ear, "Jesus will never make you rich, but his enemies could. Why not help them catch Jesus?"

How delighted the priests and Pharisees had been when Judas crept into their meeting and offered to show them where Jesus slept at night. "We'll give you thirty pieces of silver," they smiled.

But Judas did not feel very comfortable as he sat at supper that night. "He knows what I've done!" he thought as he wriggled under the steady gaze of Jesus.

"Better go and fetch the soldiers now," whispered Satan. "Tonight would be a good time, with all the people safely at home feasting."

As Judas slipped out into the night, Jesus began to break the bread and hand the pieces to his friends. Then he poured wine into a cup and gave everyone a sip. "I'm going away," he told them gently. "Every time you share bread and wine together it will remind you of me."

"Going away!" they all exclaimed in dismay.

"Don't worry," smiled Jesus, "I will come back and live in your hearts, but of course you won't be able to see me. Now we must be going; Satan is trying to have me killed. But remember, he can do nothing unless I allow it."

"No one's going to hurt you with me around!" boasted Peter, picking up his sword.

"Before you hear the cock crow in the morning, Peter," replied Jesus sadly, "you'll say three times that you never knew me."

They followed him out of the city and found the little garden Jesus loved so much.

"Something terrible's going to happen," whispered John nervously.

"We'll be safe here among the trees," yawned Peter. "No one else knows we come here at night." But he was wrong.

John 18:1-10; Mark 14:51-72; Luke 22:61-62

SOLDIERS IN THE NIGHT

JESUS WAS FRIGHTENED. He knew, as he waited in the lonely darkness of the garden, that Judas and the soldiers were on their way to arrest him. He also knew how much they would hurt him when they dragged him away.

"Father," he cried as he threw himself down on the ground, "isn't there some other way we could save people from Satan?"

He knew there was no answer his Father could give, and when he remembered how much he loved us all he dried his eyes and stood up quickly. If only he had someone to keep him company, but all his disciples were sound asleep.

Suddenly the darkness was split by torchlight. Roman soldiers and Jewish policemen surged among the trees, their swords glinting in the moonlight. "Which man do we want, Judas?" they demanded.

"This one," replied the traitor as he stepped up to Jesus and gave him a kiss.

As the Romans sprang forward to seize their prisoner, a power they could not see sent them sprawling backwards in a tangled heap. Jesus is far more powerful than Satan, and no army could have killed the Son of God if it had not been part of his plan. Peter did not realize that, so he jumped in front of Jesus, swinging his sword at the soldiers as they struggled to their feet. All he managed to do was cut off one of their ears!

Stepping forward quickly, Jesus healed the man and then allowed the soldiers to tie him up and march him back to the city.

"Run for your lives!" screamed the disciples as they disappeared in all directions. Leaping after them, the soldiers grabbed a young boy called Mark. All he was wearing was his nightshirt, but he twisted violently, slid right out of it and ran on into the darkness.

Peter did not run away. Instead he crept along in the shadows, keeping a safe distance behind the soldiers until they reached the high priest's house.

"Are you the Son of God?" demanded Caiaphas.

The angry faces of the priests and Pharisees glared at Jesus as they waited for his reply.

"I am," he answered, "and one day you will see me on my throne in heaven."

"How DARE YOU say you are the same as God!" stormed the high priest. "You shall die!"

"But only the Romans can kill prisoners," grumbled someone.

"Pilate, their governor, will soon have him crucified if he thinks this man is trying to make himself our King," smiled the Pharisees.

Outside in the courtyard, the soldiers were warming themselves by the fire. Peter slipped through the gate, trying to hear what was happening in the house.

"You're one of his friends," said someone.

"No!" answered Peter, suddenly afraid.

"Yes, you are," added someone else.

"Never seen him in my life," protested Peter.

"I've seen you with him," giggled a servant girl.

"I swear to you I don't know him!" shouted Peter—just as the cock began to crow.

Through the open doors Jesus turned and looked straight at Peter, who fled away into the dark street, crying bitterly.

THE DAY THE SUN COULD NOT SHINE

OUT OF THE CITY and up the hill marched the Roman soldiers. They had beaten Jesus with their cruel whips until he was nearly dead, but still they forced him to carry a huge, wooden cross.

"You say you're a King," they had jeered at him, "so you'd better have a crown." Out of sharp thorns they made him one, and rammed it down on his head until the blood ran down his face.

At the top of the hill, they threw him to the ground and hammered great nails through his hands and feet.

"Father," gasped Jesus, "forgive them, they don't realize what they're doing."

Up in the air swung the cross, while the soldiers threw dice to see who should have his clothes.

"You were just a liar all the time!" jeered the people as they poured out of Jerusalem to stare at Jesus hanging there. "If you really were the Son of God, you could step down from that cross."

Two other men hung on either side of Jesus; both were robbers. "Why don't you save yourself and us," mocked one of them.

"Be quiet," sobbed the other thief. "We both deserve to die for what we've done, but this man never did anything wrong. Sir, will you remember me when you rule your kingdom?"

"I am telling you the truth," gasped Jesus, "today you will be with me in heaven."

Someone was crying, and Jesus looked down and saw his mother Mary kneeling by his cross. Most of his family and friends had run away, so Jesus looked around to find someone to comfort her. There in the shadows he caught sight of John. "Look after my mother," pleaded Jesus. "And mother, care for John." Down the hill they walked together, leaving Jesus to hang there alone.

God could not watch while Jesus was blamed for our sins; He had to turn away. The sun disappeared, leaving the earth covered in an awful darkness.

In heaven waited armies of angels. If Jesus had called, they would have destroyed the whole world, but he loved us enough to go on hanging there.

Of course Satan and all his devils were dancing in triumph. They thought they had won! They did not realize that God was placing on Jesus all the bad things people have ever done, so that we do not need to die for our own sins.

Satan's power was broken at last, when in the darkness Jesus cried, "It is finished!" and allowed himself to die.

The sun came blazing out again, and the Roman soldiers stood gazing up at the cross in wonder. "This man really was the Son of God," they told each other.

Into the Roman governor's office hurried the priests. "That liar Jesus said he would come to life again," they said. "He's been buried in a cave covered with a heavy stone, but it might be safer if soldiers guarded the grave."

As Pilate gave the order, the priests smiled. "Jesus can't escape us now!" they thought, but they were going to have a great surprise!

THE EMPTY GRAVE

THROUGH THE EARLY morning shadows hurried a group of women. Tears blinded them as they neared the garden where Jesus was buried.

"I may feel better when I know his body is properly wrapped," thought one of them, who was called Mary Magdalene. "Without Jesus, nothing will ever make me happy again." No one had ever loved Mary, until the day Jesus had touched her and changed her life.

"However shall we move that heavy stone," sighed the women.

They need not have worried, because just before they arrived something marvelous had happened. A shining angel rolled away the great stone and Jesus himself walked out of the cave. The soldiers were so terrified they fainted as the ground rumbled and shook.

When the women arrived, all they saw was an empty tomb. "Where are the soldiers?" they gasped.

At that moment the soldiers were banging on the high priest's door and their teeth were chattering with terror. "He's g-g-g-gone!" they spluttered. "An angel moved the stone, and out he came."

"We'll pay you anything you like," pleaded the priests, "but don't tell anyone! Just say his friends stole the body while you slept."

"We can't do that!" protested the soldiers. "Pilate would have us crucified."

"We'll see you're safe," the priests promised.

Nervously, some of the women stepped into the cave and found it filled with silvery light. "Why do you look inside a grave for someone who is alive?" asked the angel who was sitting there. "Don't you remember how Jesus was always telling you he would become alive again?"

The women rushed back to the city to tell the disciples, but Mary Magdalene just could not believe in angels. "Those soldiers have taken him," she sobbed, pressing her face against the cold stone.

Suddenly she could feel someone standing behind her. "Perhaps it's the gardener," she thought. "Sir, do YOU know where they've taken him?" she demanded.

"Mary." Only one person ever spoke her name like that. Rubbing the tears from her eyes she spun around and gazed into the face of Jesus. "Go and tell the others I'm alive," he said gently.

The doors of the upstairs room were locked and the windows boarded up. The frightened disciples were all hiding together from the Pharisees.

"All day long, people have been bursting in here, saying they've seen strange things," muttered Peter. "But we all know Jesus has gone away forever."

"But I saw him," protested Mary Magdalene for the hundredth time.

Just then two men hammered on the door, their faces red and hot from running. "The women are right!" they panted. "We've seen Jesus too! We were walking home this evening when we met a man who reminded us that the prophets have always said the Messiah would die and then rise again. God's plan has NOT gone wrong after all! We asked him in for the night and, as we sat eating, suddenly we knew it was Jesus, so we ran back to tell you!"

"We just can't believe all this," protested the others miserably.

The door was tightly closed, but that did not stop Jesus from walking straight through it and, at that moment, there he was, smiling at them all.

"I'm hungry," he said. "What's for supper?"

Matthew 28:16-20; Mark 16:14-20; Luke 24:45-52; John 21; Acts 1:1-11

PICNIC BREAKFAST

"I FEEL LIKE A LION shut in a cage!" growled Peter as he prowled around the little room where the disciples were still hiding.

"But Jesus often comes to see us," soothed John. "We've all seen him lots of times now."

"Yes, but I need to feel a boat under my feet and the sea spray in my face," replied Peter. "I'm going back to fishing."

Several of the others went with him, but things did not go as Peter had planned. "I just can't believe this!" he exclaimed, because all night long they caught nothing at all.

Then through the early morning mist they saw a man standing on the beach, and his voice carried clearly over the calm water. "Let the nets down on the RIGHT side of the boat."

"That's what Jesus said once," smiled Peter as he heaved at the heavy fishing nets. At once, the whole boat sprang to life. Fish were everywhere; the nets bulged with them.

"That must be the Lord himself," gasped John, but Peter did not wait to agree. Over the side and into the water he dived. If Jesus was there on the beach, he wanted to be near him.

A driftwood fire was crackling by the water's edge and bread and fish were laid out ready for breakfast. But all Peter could do was gaze at Jesus in amazement.

"Peter, do you love me?" asked Jesus quietly.

"Of course!" choked Peter.

"Then look after my friends."

It was later, when the others had dragged the net ashore, that Jesus asked again, "Peter, do you love me?"

"You know I do," protested Peter.

"Then teach my followers," smiled Jesus. "But Peter, are you SURE you love me?" Suddenly Peter remembered the terrible night when he said three times that he had never known Jesus, and his face turned red with shame. "You know everything, Lord," he said. "You know I love you."

"That's why I need you to care for the others," said Jesus as he put his hand on Peter's shoulder.

"I'll never go back to fishing," promised Peter. "I'll spend my life telling people about you."

"That's what I want you all to do," said Jesus turning to the others. "Go EVERYWHERE in the world and tell all the people that I love them. Explain that they can come close to God and live forever in heaven because I died for them. All the people have to do is be sorry for the bad things they do and let me help them to change."

Then, as he looked around at them all, he added, "Don't ever forget, I will always be with you."

That did seem a strange thing to say, when a little time later they went for a walk with Jesus in the hills near Jerusalem. Suddenly the whole sky was full of golden glory and Jesus began to rise up into the air. "I am going back to my Father," he called. "Stay in Jerusalem and wait until I come to live with you forever by my Spirit."

He came to earth as a tiny baby in a dirty stable, but he left on clouds of shining light. The angels sang and shouted their welcome while the disciples fell down on their faces to worship him. They did not realize just then that their adventures were only just beginning!

189

THE ADVENTURE BEGINS

THE WAITING SEEMED so long. There they all were, crammed together in the upstairs room, frightened of the priests and lonely without Jesus. Yet as they read the old books of the Bible their excitement grew as they saw how God had been working out his secret plan right from the very beginning.

Then, early one morning when everyone who loved Jesus had squeezed into the room to pray to him, something wonderful happened. A noise like a great storm filled the room and flames of fire seemed to dance about their heads. God Himself, by His Spirit, entered each of them and made them strong and brave.

They burst open the locked doors and rushed out into the street. Jerusalem was full of people who had traveled up to the feast and soon they were crowding around the disciples listening to their story.

"You all remember Jesus of Nazareth and the amazing things he did," yelled Peter. "You had him crucified, but God raised him from death because he's really our God and King!"

As they listened to Peter, they could all understand him in their own languages, and thousands believed in Jesus and became his disciples that very day. Soon they were all spending their time learning more and more about Jesus.

One day, as Peter and John hurried through the temple gates, a lame beggar tugged at Peter's coat. "Spare a coin, sir," he pleaded.

"I have no money," replied Peter kindly, "but what I do have is yours. In the name of Jesus, stand up." The man had never walked in his life and now he was old. Yet he jumped to his feet and began to dance around, wild with excitement. Soon a vast crowd had gathered, staring in amazement.

"I did not heal this man," laughed Peter; "it was the power of Jesus of Nazareth flowing through me."

Soon many more people had made Jesus King of their lives, but just then a group of furious priests arrived and pushed their way to the front of the crowd. "Take these troublemakers to prison!" they ordered the police.

The next morning Caiaphas the high priest let the two disciples go, after telling them never to mention Jesus again. Peter smiled because he knew he could never promise that.

There were soon so many new disciples in Jerusalem they could hardly be counted, and once again the priests had their twelve leaders (who were now called apostles) thrown into prison. "We've got them this time," they said, but in the night angels came and set them free.

When the police opened the prison door in the morning the cell was empty. "They've gone!" they told the priests.

"No they haven't," snapped Caiaphas, "they're already in the temple preaching."

"How can we stop this dreadful business?" they asked each other.

"We should whip them so hard they won't even dare to THINK of Jesus," growled Caiaphas.

So that is what they tried to do, but the apostles were happy to think they could suffer for Jesus, and with him alive inside them they were afraid of nothing.

THE MAN WHO HATED JESUS

"THESE PEOPLE must be stopped!" roared the high priest. All the important men of Jerusalem had been called to his house for a special meeting. "Things are becoming serious," Caiaphas continued. "Thousands of people think this Jesus is actually God; they even believe he lives inside them!"

"Their leaders do the same kind of amazing miracles this Jesus did," added another priest. "I've arrested one of them, a man called Stephen; he's outside now."

Stephen had never done anything except love and help people, so the priests had to make up lies about him. Standing listening was a young Pharisee called Saul. He believed those lies, and became so angry he ground his teeth with rage. Then Stephen looked up and exclaimed, "I can see right into heaven and Jesus is standing there beside God." Everyone in the room jumped to their feet screaming with rage.

"How could Jesus be the same as God?" thought Saul angrily as he watched Stephen being dragged outside the city gate to be stoned to death.

"Hold our coats, Saul," ordered the Jews, and soon sharp rocks were whizzing towards Stephen from all directions.

All he could see around him were faces full of hate, but he remembered that Jesus had told him to love his enemies. So as the cruel stones battered his head, he prayed, "Lord, please don't be angry with them for this."

"I'll spend the rest of my life destroying every follower of this Jesus," vowed Saul as he watched Stephen die.

From that very day, terrible things began to happen in Jerusalem. Saul marched around with soldiers searching every house, dragging out men, women and even children.

He whipped them, put them in prison or had them killed. He thought he was so clever, but the disciples who escaped from Jerusalem went all over the country telling people about Jesus. Soon thousands more believed in him.

"You're making things worse, Saul," grumbled Caiaphas. "I've heard there are hundreds of them in Damascus now."

"Then I'll go there and drag them back in chains!" growled Saul.

The disciples in Damascus were terrified when they heard Saul was coming. "We can't SEE Jesus any more," said their leader, "but we can still TALK to him and ask for his help."

Along the road marched Saul, muttering threats with every step. He could see Damascus in the distance, when suddenly a burning light knocked him to the ground.

"Saul, why do you hate me?" came a voice from the sky.

"Who are you, Lord?" gasped Saul as he lay in the dust.

"I am Jesus, the one you are fighting."

Saul's soldiers rushed to help him, but as he staggered to his feet they saw that his eyes were blinded.

The disciples in Damascus were amazed when they saw the man they had feared so much being lead into the city by the hand, just like a little child.

DARING ESCAPES

ANANIAS WAS AN old man and he did NOT want to go to prison. Like all the other disciples in Damascus he was praying hard that God would save him from Saul. Early one morning, he suddenly heard Jesus say, "Ananias, go to Straight Street. I have told a man there, called Saul, that you are coming to heal his eyes."

"SAUL!" exclaimed Ananias. "Lord, I'm too frightened of that man to go near him!"

"Go," replied Jesus, "because I have chosen him to tell the world who I am."

Saul was kneeling in a darkened room. For three days he had eaten nothing as he cried to God to forgive him. When Ananias touched his eyes, he could see again, and then the old man took him to meet the other astonished followers of Jesus.

Saul was so different after he had met Jesus on the road that day; even his name was changed to Paul. Soon he was telling the Jews in Damascus that Jesus was their Messiah. "We must kill this wicked man!" they cried.

"Escape quickly," the disciples told Paul. "They are watching the gates, but tonight we will hide you in a basket and let you down over the city walls on a rope."

Away into the darkness ran Paul, but when he arrived in Jerusalem he had a nasty surprise. The apostles were terrified when he asked to see them.

"This is just his new trick to catch us," said Peter. Poor Paul; he was desperately lonely. His old friends were angry with him and the followers of Jesus would not trust him. Then Barnabas, a very kind disciple, believed his story at last and took him to Peter.

Paul was soon preaching all over Jerusalem and helping many people to know Jesus.

Then a dreadful thing happened. King Herod arrested Peter. "Guard this man well," he told the soldiers. "Tomorrow he will die."

The disciples were devastated. Jesus had told Peter to look after them. How could they possibly manage without him? "We must pray," they decided as they crammed into a house belonging to Mark's mother.

Peter was not at all worried. He knew Jesus had died to make it possible for him to go to heaven, so he settled down to sleep, chained to his guards. Suddenly someone was shaking him and he woke to find the dungeon full of light. "Dress quickly," whispered an angel, as the chains slithered from Peter's hands and feet.

"I'm dreaming," yawned Peter as he followed the angel past rows of soldiers. But as the cold, night air stung his face he realized he was outside the castle and the heavy prison door was swinging shut behind him. The angel was gone, and Peter found himself alone in the dark street.

Like a chariot horse he raced to Mark's
house and banged on the door. Inside they
were too busy praying to notice. "I'll be
caught again in a minute," thought Peter
desperately as he knocked again.

At last a little servant girl called Rhoda
peeped out of the window. She was so
surprised she ran back into the prayer
meeting. "Peter's outside!" she gasped.

"Be quiet," they said crossly. "How could
he be?" But Peter was still knocking, and
how astonished they were when at last
they opened the door!

THE MAN FROM AFRICA

THE EMPRESS OF Ethiopia sat on her throne looking sad. "Mr. Secretary of the Treasury," she said, "you must go to Jerusalem and find out about the God of the Jews."

"But Madam," he gasped, "Jerusalem is so far from Africa and away across the desert!"

"You shall have soldiers to protect you and my best chariot," she replied. "Leave at once."

When the treasurer of Ethiopia finally arrived in Jerusalem, he went immediately to the temple. He asked many questions but the answers puzzled him completely. "These Pharisees don't know God at all," he thought at last. "Coming here was a waste of time."

Then he bought himself a book to read on his long journey home and climbed sadly back into his chariot.

Philip, an evangelist and one of the seven deacons, had escaped from Jerusalem to a city in Samaria. As soon as he began to tell the people there about Jesus, thousands of them listened to him everyday.

"Soon they'll all be followers of Jesus," he thought happily. Then suddenly, in the middle of the eager crowds, God told Philip to do a very strange thing. "Go into the desert," He said. "I've got a job for you to do."

"A job? Here?" grumbled Philip as he trudged along the lonely road that led to Africa. All he could see was miles of sand. "I left behind thousands of people in Samaria," he thought, "but I can't tell anyone about Jesus in this lonely place."

Just then, in the distance, he saw a cloud of dust. The chariots and horses of the treasurer of Ethiopia were approaching like a whirlwind at high speed.

"Go with those people," said God.

"The desert's too hot for a job like this!" puffed poor Philip as he sprinted along.

The treasurer was so busy reading he did not see Philip running beside him. The book had been written hundreds of years before by Isaiah the prophet. The words were all about Jesus and they puzzled the treasurer completely. "Who IS this man who was punished instead of me?" he muttered. "Bruised and beaten so I could go free?"

"Do you understand what you're reading?" panted Philip through the swirling dust.

"How can I?" snapped the treasurer. "No one will explain it to me." Then peering more closely at Philip he added, "You're a Jew, perhaps you can help. Jump in beside me."

When Philip was settled in the chariot, the treasurer demanded, "Who is this man who was treated so cruelly?"

"My friend Jesus!" beamed Philip, and as they rode over the desert he told the Ethiopian the whole story of God's secret plan.

"Look! We are coming to an oasis!" said the treasurer that evening. "Couldn't I be baptized, to show my sins are washed away?"

As he stepped from the water his face was beaming with joy, and he said, "Now I can go home to Africa and tell my queen and all her people this good news." And that is exactly what he did!

197

OFF AROUND THE WORLD

BRICKS AND STONES came whizzing towards him. Paul dodged this way and that, but he knew it was no use; the angry people of Lystra were determined to kill him.

As the stones beat him to the pavement he remembered Stephen and how he had watched him stoned to death like this. "I'll be in heaven with him too, any moment now," thought Paul.

While he had been in Jerusalem, God had spoken to Paul and told him a new part of his secret plan. God loved EVERYONE in the world, not just Jews. He had sent Jesus to show people everywhere what he was like and to die so anyone could go to heaven. "I want you to travel the world telling everyone this good news!" God told Paul. So that is what he and his friend Barnabas had been doing.

Whenever they arrived in a city they always asked first if there were any Jews living there. If they would not believe their Messiah had come, then Paul would stand in the streets and say, "God loves YOU, Romans, Greeks, Africans and Indians JUST as much as he loves us Jews." That made the Jews furious.

"God only loves US!" they raged in a place called Iconium. "We're not having any of these new 'Christians' here," and they chased Paul and Barnabas from their city.

The first person they saw when they arrived in the next town was a lame beggar crouching in the marketplace. "We're here to tell you people of Lystra about someone called Jesus," said Paul. "He can make people well, even that lame beggar who has never walked in his life."

As the man jumped to his feet the people of the town stood with their mouths open in astonishment. "These men must be gods, come down from the sky," they whispered.

In that land they believed in hundreds of pretend gods, and outside Lystra stood a huge temple to one they called 'Zeus'. Paul and Barnabas were horrified when they saw the doors open and all the priests of Zeus come running out with their dancing girls to decorate the two friends with garlands of flowers. "We will offer you sacrifices of our best bulls," the people said as they bowed low to the ground.

"NO! NO!" shouted Paul and Barnabas in horror. "We are just ordinary men like you. You mustn't kneel to us. We came to tell you about the REAL God. You should worship HIM!"

Just at that moment, a group of Jews hurried into the city. They had followed Paul and Barnabus from Iconium. "Don't listen to these men!" they shouted as they pushed their way through the cheering crowds. "They're liars and troublemakers!"

It was then that the people of Lystra began to stone Paul.

"Throw him out of the city," snarled the priests of Zeus when they saw Paul was dead. "Let the birds eat his body."

That night, Barnabas and some of the other believers in Jesus crept out to bury Paul. But as they stood around his bleeding body, he suddenly opened his eyes and smiled at them. He had not been killed after all.

Soon the two friends were on their way to the next city, leaving behind them in Lystra a new group of believers—now known as "Christians."

THE FORTUNE-TELLER

THE EARTHQUAKE happened in Philippi. Paul traveled to the city with another of his friends, Silas. Many people there were excited to hear about Jesus and wanted to be his followers. Everything would have been wonderful if it had not been for the fortune-teller.

Satan lived in this girl, just as the Spirit of Jesus lives in his followers. God's enemy helped her to see into the future and she could tell people just what was going to happen to them.

Some men of the city had made her their slave, and they were becoming rich by charging people a lot of money to hear their fortunes.

As soon as this poor girl saw Paul and Silas, the evil spirit inside her was afraid of them. She began to shout and make a dreadful noise.

Paul felt so sorry for her that in the end he could stand it no longer and commanded Satan to leave her completely. Suddenly the girl felt happy and free for the first time in her life, but she could no longer see into the future.

The men who owned her were so furious they dragged Paul and Silas in front of the mayor of Philippi. "These men are causing trouble in our city," they shouted. So Roman soldiers tied Paul and Silas to the whipping posts and beat them with their cruel whips.

"Jailer!" shouted the magistrates. "Keep these men safe in your prison; if they escape you will die!"

It was the middle of the night. Paul and Silas were in too much pain to sleep. Their feet were locked into wooden holes called stocks and their backs were bruised and bleeding. They were hungry and cold and the prison was very dark.

"Come on, Silas," said Paul. "We'll sing some hymns to praise God." All the other prisoners listened in amazement. What kind of men could sing in a place like this?

Just then the Roman fort began to rattle and shake. The stone walls cracked and the prison door fell off its hinges. An earthquake ripped the chains from their hands and freed their feet from the stocks.

Paul and Silas were just about to step outside to freedom when they saw the terrified jailer. He did not want to be killed by the Romans, so he picked up his sword and pointed it towards his own heart.

"No!" shouted Paul. "Don't hurt yourself; no one has escaped."

Calling for a light, the jailer bounded towards them and threw himself down before Paul and Silas. "Sirs, what must I do to be saved?"

"Believe in Jesus," replied Paul gently.

That night the jailer and all his family became Christians, and carefully they bathed the wounded backs of Paul and Silas, gave them food and took them home to sleep in comfortable beds.

The next day the magistrates actually came themselves to say they were sorry for treating them so badly, and when Paul had taught the little group of new Christians many things, he and Silas traveled on to their next adventure.

THE GODDESS DIANA

PAUL WHISTLED happily as he worked. For two years now he had stayed in the great city of Ephesus, making tents and sharing his little house with his great friends, the doctor Luke, Gaius and Aristarchus.

Hundreds of people flocked to hear Paul preach during lunch hour every day, and many became Christians.

Through his workshop window Paul could see the huge temple of the goddess Diana. People used to come from all over the world to worship the idol they said had dropped out of the sky. "But now the Lord Jesus has broken the power of Diana and all her witches and magicians," smiled Paul.

Just then the door burst open and in rushed Luke. "There's trouble in the city!" he panted.

"Why?" asked Paul. "More people are becoming Christians every day."

"That's why there's trouble!" replied the doctor. "A man called Demetrius has called a meeting for all the shopkeepers and hotel-owners. They are saying you have spoiled their trade. So many people have become Christians, they no longer come here to worship Diana and spend money in the town."

"Demetrius makes little silver images of Diana and sells them for a high price," chuckled Paul. "People are beginning to realize it's useless praying to an idol, so he can't sell so many!"

"Don't laugh, Paul," warned Luke. "You are in great danger. Demetrius has called the whole city together into the arena. There's going to be a riot."

Most Roman cities had a place like a football stadium where everyone went to watch chariot racing, and thousands of Ephesians were crowding there now.

"I must go too and speak to the crowds," said Paul.

"NO!" said some of his friends as they hurried in. "The crowds will kill you. Demetrius has already caught Gaius and Aristarchus and dragged them to the arena."

"We all became rich because of our goddess Diana," shouted Demetrius from the middle of the arena. "This Paul tells people she's only a model. If we don't stop him soon, we won't have any money left at all!"

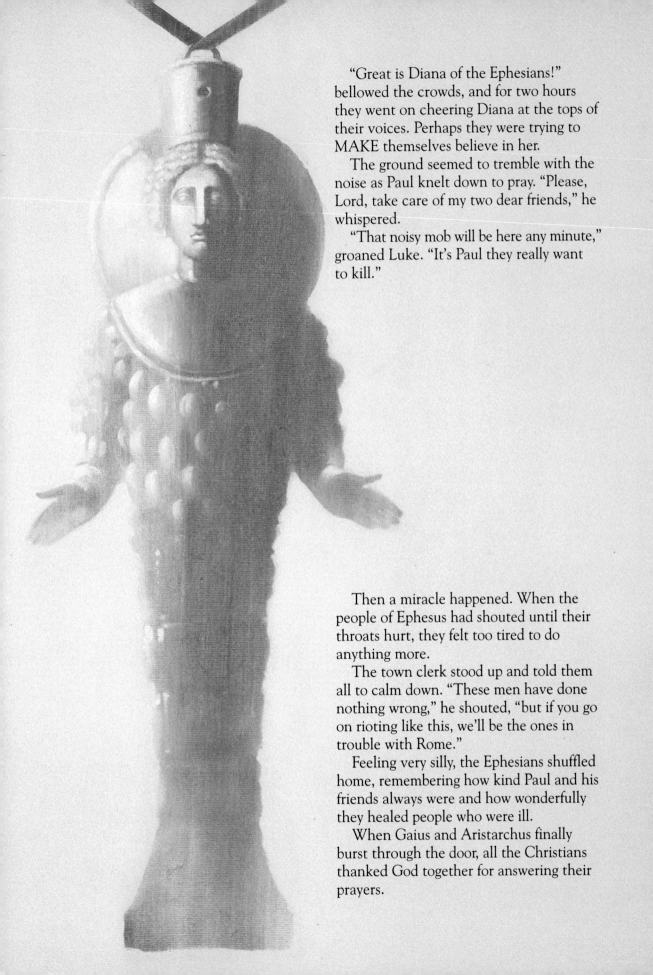

"Great is Diana of the Ephesians!" bellowed the crowds, and for two hours they went on cheering Diana at the tops of their voices. Perhaps they were trying to MAKE themselves believe in her.

The ground seemed to tremble with the noise as Paul knelt down to pray. "Please, Lord, take care of my two dear friends," he whispered.

"That noisy mob will be here any minute," groaned Luke. "It's Paul they really want to kill."

Then a miracle happened. When the people of Ephesus had shouted until their throats hurt, they felt too tired to do anything more.

The town clerk stood up and told them all to calm down. "These men have done nothing wrong," he shouted, "but if you go on rioting like this, we'll be the ones in trouble with Rome."

Feeling very silly, the Ephesians shuffled home, remembering how kind Paul and his friends always were and how wonderfully they healed people who were ill.

When Gaius and Aristarchus finally burst through the door, all the Christians thanked God together for answering their prayers.

THE SHIPWRECK

HOW DARE THIS man come here," thundered the high priest. For many years Paul had been traveling the world teaching thousands of people about Jesus. Now he was back in Jerusalem to tell the apostles all his adventures. That made the Jews furious; they hated Paul for saying God loved even people who weren't Jews.

Soon a mob of angry Jews gathered around Paul in the temple and began to try to beat him to death.

Down the stairs from the castle streamed the Roman soldiers, and they dragged Paul back up to safety.

"This man has done nothing wrong," they said after they had kept Paul in prison for two years. He had spent his time writing to all the groups of new Christians or churches which he had started around the world, and these letters are now part of our Bible today.

"We want him to die," snarled the Jews.

"We'll see what our emperor thinks about him," replied the Romans and put Paul and his friend Luke on a boat bound for Rome.

"I've always longed to visit the Christians in Rome," smiled Paul. But Luke wasn't listening; he was too busy writing a book all about Jesus and another about Paul and the other apostles. Luke's books are in our Bible too.

One day, they reached a harbor on the island of Cyprus. The Roman officer who was in charge of all the prisoners on the ship was talking to the captain. "Perhaps it would be safer if we stayed here for the winter," he was saying.

"No," argued the captain, "we should sail on farther."

"Excuse me." Both men spun around to stare at Paul. "We SHOULD stay here," he warned. "God says terrible winds will destroy this ship if we go on."

But the Roman officer would not listen to a mere prisoner, and soon they were sailing out to sea.

But he SHOULD have listened. A dreadful hurricane began to batter the ship. Great waves crashed against its sides and lightning hit the mast.

In those days sailors found their way by looking at the sun and stars, but the rain clouds darkened the sky and soon the captain had no idea where they were.

For days they struggled to keep the boat afloat and everyone was terrified, except the two Christians.

At last Paul stood up and shouted above the shrieking wind, "Don't be frightened; I am God's servant, and last night he told me we shall all be safe. Now you must eat something to make you strong again, for soon we shall be washed up on an island."

Almost at once, the ship stuck on a sandbar and began to break up completely. Everyone jumped into the water and, clinging to pieces of the broken ship, they were swept onto a beach.

"Make a fire," ordered the Roman officer. "We're wet and frozen." Some of the islanders were helping them collect wood when a snake darted out and bit Paul's hand. "He'll die now," everyone whispered, but Paul just shook the snake away—he knew Jesus would heal him.

Soon everyone on the island of Malta was learning about Jesus and being healed by his power. Months later, when Paul sailed for Rome, he left behind many new Christians.

THE HAPPY PRISONER

THE WIND AND WAVES beat against the little island, but the prisoner in the castle was too busy writing to notice.

John was a very old man now, but he remembered so well the day he had looked up from his fishing nets and first seen Jesus. He had already written about those days in a book that is now part of the Bible.

Now all the other apostles were dead. Peter and Paul had died bravely in Rome; John's own brother, James, had been killed by King Herod, and many of the others had died in prison because they would not stop telling people about Jesus.

John was not sad or lonely, because of a wonderful thing that had happened to him there, in prison, one Sunday morning. Jesus had actually appeared in his cell. He did not look dusty, tired and shabby as he had so often looked before. His clothes shone and his eyes blazed like fire.

The old man was so surprised he fell to the ground, but the voice he remembered and loved so much said to him gently, "Don't be afraid, John. I WAS dead, but now I live forever. I want to show you what is going to happen so you can write it all down in a book, which will make everyone who reads it full of joy."

Then John was allowed to see right into heaven. It was all so beautiful he couldn't think of enough words to describe it. "How happy all these people look," he gasped as he gazed around.

"They are all the people who have loved God since the world began," said Jesus. "And now they will be happy for ever. No one has to say 'goodbye' in heaven. People are never lonely or sad, and death will never part them from the people they love. No pain or illness is allowed here or darkness to make them afraid. I have wiped their tears away forever."

But not everyone was happy. John saw Satan and everyone who obeyed him thrown into a lake of everlasting fire. "Never again will Satan spoil God's plans," said Jesus. "He is beaten forever."

John shivered and looked rather frightened, so Jesus showed him a great book full of names. "When someone decides to follow me and asks to become my disciple, their name is written here for ever in the Book of Life," explained Jesus. "No one can ever rub it out; they are safe forever. Now go and write about all these things so no one need ever again be frightened of dying."

John put down his pen and smiled as he leaned back in his chair. When he thought about heaven and all the wonderful things he had seen there, he could not help remembering something

Jesus had said years before: "For God loved the world so much, he gave his only Son, that whoever believes in him should not die, but live forever!"

That had been God's great plan even since he had first made the world, and with a happy sigh John went on with his writing.